SCOTT FORESMAN • ADDISON WESLEY

Mathematics

Grades K–2

Math Games Teaching Guide

Editorial Offices: Glenview, Illinois • Parsippany, New Jersey • New York, New York

Sales Offices: Parsippany, New Jersey • Duluth, Georgia • Glenview, Illinois
Coppell, Texas • Ontario, California • Mesa, Arizona

How to Use the Games

Math Games provide students with a fun way to practice mathematical skills. On page iv you will find a correlation of the games to the content of the chapters in Grades K–2 of Scott Foresman-Addison Wesley Mathematics. At least one game per chapter is included.

Many of the games use a board. Nine boards are included in the K–2 Math Games packet, each with two colorful game boards printed back-to-back. Most games have game cards, which are provided in this Teaching Guide. Each game also includes a list of materials and directions, and many have an answer key. The pages in this Teaching Guide are meant to be reproduced.

At these grade levels, the reading ability of children should be evaluated in order to determine their capacity to play the games on their own. Children who read well and work independently can be provided with a copy of the directions and the answer key to use as they play the game. It may be helpful to explain the directions to all the children the first time they play a game.

In addition to more guidance in playing the game, Kindergarten children and some children in Grades 1 and 2 should be provided with manipulatives instead of an answer key to check the answers. If appropriate for the game, manipulatives will be listed in the materials section as options to the answer key. Children may also use manipulatives to help them solve the problems.

Game cards for a particular game appear on the pages following the answer key, if any, for that game. These pages should be reproduced and cut apart along the dotted lines.

On the backside of the game cards for The Farm, Prehistoric Animals, Sky-High, Deep-Sea Diver, Farmer's Market, and Shell Facts is a picture. When a child correctly answers the question on a game card, he or she places the card on the board, question-side down, so that a portion of the picture is revealed. As the game progresses, the picture is completed. Instructions for creating these two-sided game cards are included with each game.

ISBN: 0-328-08118-3

2 3 4 5 6 7 8 9 10 -V084- 09 08 07 06 05 04 03

Table of Contents

Correlation

Game	Content	Kindergarten	Grade 1	Grade 2
Same Shape	Match Shapes	Use anytime after Chapter 1, Lesson 1-5.		
The Zoo	Identify Groups and Recognize Numbers	Use anytime after Chapter 3, Lesson 3-1.		
Pattern Party	Create Patterns with Two or More Repetitions	Use anytime after Chapter 2, Lesson 2-10.	Use anytime after Chapter 1, Lesson 1-3.	
Leap Frog	Compare Numbers to 10	Use anytime after Chapter 4, Lesson 4-7.	Use anytime after Chapter 1, Lesson 1-11.	
Fewer and Fewer	Subtract 1 or 2 to Make New Numbers	Use anytime after Chapter 9, Lesson 9-7.	Use anytime after Chapter 1, Lesson 1-10.	
Prehistoric Animals	Sequence Numbers through 31	Use anytime after Chapter 5, Lesson 5-7.	Use anytime after Chapter 7, Lesson 7-3.	Use anytime after Chapter 3, Lesson 3-7.
Inchworm	Measure Length	Use anytime after Chapter 6, Lesson 6-5.	Use anytime after Chapter 10, Lesson 10-1.	Use anytime after Chapter 9, Lesson 9-1.
The Farm	Tell Time to the Hour	Use anytime after Chapter 7, Lesson 7-7.	Use anytime after Chapter 6, Lesson 6-3.	Use anytime after Chapter 8, Lesson 8-1.
Name That Shape	Identify Shapes	Use anytime after Chapter 8, Lesson 8-5.	Use anytime after Chapter 5, Lesson 5-4.	Use anytime after Chapter 7, Lesson 7-2.
Sky-High	Add 0, 1, 2, or 3 to a Number	Use anytime after Chap. 10, Lesson 10-6.	Use anytime after Chapter 3, Lesson 3-3.	Use anytime after Chapter 2, Lesson 2-1.
Bubble Mania	Subtract from 10 or Less	Use anytime after Chap. 11, Lesson 11-6.	Use anytime after Chapter 4, Lesson 4-6.	Use anytime after Chapter 2, Lesson 2-8.
Fast Count	Skip Count to 100	Use anytime after Chap. 12, Lesson 12-5.	Use anytime after Chapter 7, Lesson 7-8.	Use anytime after Chapter 3, Lesson 3-8.
The Bear Facts	Add and Subtract through 10		Use anytime after Chapter 2, Lesson 2-9.	Use anytime after Chapter 1, Lesson 1-10.
Fraction Fun	Recognize Fractions		Use anytime after Chapter 5, Lesson 5-12.	Use anytime after Chapter 7, Lesson 7-10.
Time's Up	Tell Time to the Half Hour		Use anytime after Chapter 6, Lesson 6-4.	Use anytime after Chapter 8, Lesson 8-1.
High-Rise Math	Identify Ordinal Numbers to Tenth		Use anytime after Chapter 7, Lesson 7-12.	Use anytime after Chapter 3, Lesson 3-10.
Picking Favorites	Understand Bar Graphs		Use anytime after Chapter 8, Lesson 8-13.	Use anytime after Chapter 8, Lesson 8-13.
Shopping Spree	Match Coin Values to Prices		Use anytime after Chapter 9, Lesson 9-7.	Use anytime after Chapter 3, Lesson 3-14.
Strawberry Patch Stories	Estimate Weight and Capacity		Use anytime after Chap. 10, Lesson 10-13.	Use anytime after Chapter 9, Lesson 9-12.
All Aboard	Add and Subtract through 18		Use anytime after Chap. 11, Lesson 11-12.	Use anytime after Chapter 2, Lesson 2-10.
Deep-Sea Diver	Add or Subtract with 2-Digit Numbers		Use anytime after Chap. 12, Lesson 12-8.	Use anytime after Chapter 4, Lesson 4-6.
Farmer's Market	Add 2-Digit Nos. with and Without Regrouping			Use anytime after Chapter 5, Lesson 5-4.
Subzero Subtraction	Subtract 2-Digit Nos. with and Without Regrouping			Use anytime after Chapter 6, Lesson 6-4.
Tic, Tac, Snow!	Order Numbers to 999			Use anytime after Chap. 10, Lesson 10-8.
Gift Boxes	Add and Subtract Money			Use anytime after Chap. 11, after Enrichment.
Shell Facts	Add and Multiply Equal Groups			Use anytime after Chap. 12, Lesson 12-2.

Same Shape

Objective: To reinforce the skill of identifying and sorting objects by shape

Use with Kindergarten anytime after Chapter 1, Lesson 1-5.

You Will Need

Same Shape game cards (36)
Same Shape answer key
1 number cube

How to Start

Two Players

Each player tosses the number cube. The player who tosses the greater number is Player 1 and starts the game.

Player 2 mixes the game cards and places them in a pile facedown on the table.

Each player takes five cards and places them faceup in front of himself or herself.

How to Play

Same Shape is a matching game.

Player 1 takes the top card from the card pile and looks to see if it matches any of his or her cards. A match is made when a picture on one card matches a picture on another card.

If Player 1 makes a match, Player 2 checks the match. If the match is correct, Player 1 picks up both cards that make the pair and puts them aside. Then Player 1 takes another game card from the card pile to replace the missing card in front of him or her.

If Player 1 does not make a match with the first card, that card is placed faceup to begin a discard pile.

It is now Player 2's turn. Player 2 may take the top game card from the card pile or the top game card from the discard pile to make a match.

Players take turns.

The game ends when there are no cards left.The winner is the player with more pairs at the end of the game.

Answer Key: Same Shape

Card	matches	Card
1.		27.
2.		25.
3.		28.
4.		35.
5.		29.
6.		33.
7.		32.
8.		26.
9.		34.
10.		19.
11.		24.
12.		30.
13.		22.
14.		31.
15.		23.
16.		20.
17.		21.
18.		36.

Variation

Players turn game cards facedown on the table. They take turns trying to make a pair. Each player turns over two cards. If the cards match, the player keeps the pair. If the cards do not match, the cards are returned to the same place with the picture kept facedown.

1.

Same Shape

2.

Same Shape

3.

Same Shape

4.

Same Shape

5.

Same Shape

6.

Same Shape

7.

Same Shape

8.

Same Shape

9.

Same Shape

10.

Same Shape

11.

Same Shape

12.

Same Shape

13.

Same Shape

14.

Same Shape

15.

Same Shape

16.

Same Shape

17.

Same Shape

18.

Same Shape

19.

Same Shape

20.

Same Shape

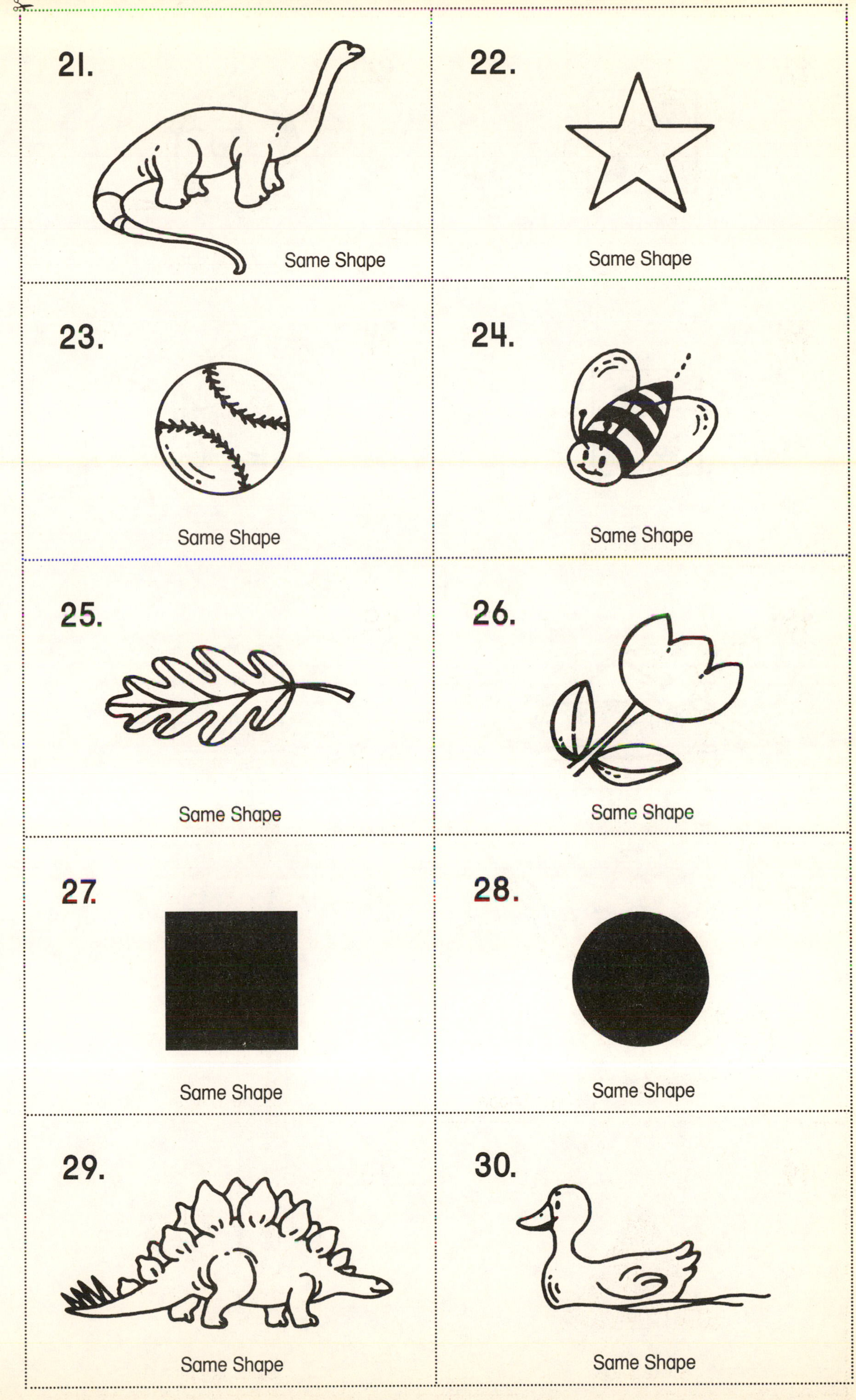
21.
Same Shape
22.
Same Shape
23.
Same Shape
24.
Same Shape
25.
Same Shape
26.
Same Shape
27.
Same Shape
28.
Same Shape
29.
Same Shape
30.
Same Shape

31.

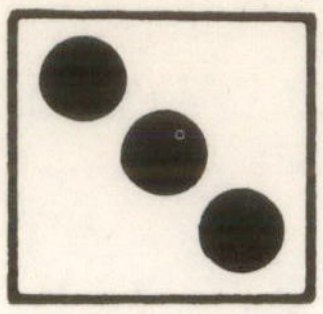

Same Shape

32.

Same Shape

33.

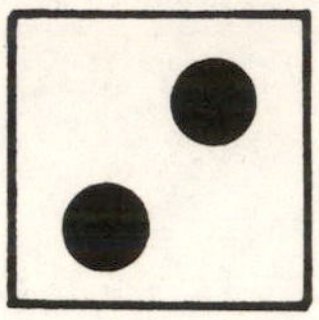

Same Shape

34.

Same Shape

35.

Same Shape

36.

Same Shape

The Zoo

Objective: To reinforce the skills of identifying groups of 1, 2, 3 and recognizing the numbers 1, 2, 3

Use with Kindergarten anytime after Chapter 3, Lesson 3-1.

You Will Need

The Zoo game board

The Zoo game cards (18)

The Zoo answer key
or counters (3 for each player)

1 number cube

18 round markers in 2 colors
(9 of each color)

How to Start

Two Players

Each player tosses the number cube. The player who tosses the greater number is Player 1 and starts the game. (Assist children as needed when determining the greater number.)

Player 2 mixes the game cards and places them facedown in a card pile on the green rectangle on the game board.

Each player starts with 9 markers of 1 color.

How to Play

The Zoo is played like tic-tac-toe.

Player 1 takes the top card from the card pile on the green rectangle, counts the animals, and tells how many he or she sees.

Player 2 uses the answer key or counters to check if Player 1's answer is correct. If it is correct, Player 1 looks for a matching number square on his or her zoo grid on the game board, and puts a marker on it.

If the answer is not correct, no marker is put down.

Then the card is placed facedown on the red rectangle, and it is Player 2's turn.

Players take turns. If all of the cards on the green rectangle are used, the cards on the red rectangle are mixed, placed facedown on the green rectangle, and used again.

The winner is the first player to put three markers across, down, or diagonally on his or her zoo grid.

Answer Key: The Zoo

1. 1	7. 2	13. 1
2. 3	8. 3	14. 2
3. 1	9. 3	15. 1
4. 2	10. 3	16. 2
5. 3	11. 1	17. 1
6. 2	12. 2	18. 3

Variation

Players can write the number on paper and then match it to the number square on his or her grid.

1.
The Zoo
2.
The Zoo
3.
The Zoo
4.
The Zoo
5.
The Zoo
6.
The Zoo
7.
The Zoo
8.
The Zoo
9.
The Zoo
10.
The Zoo

11.
The Zoo
12.
The Zoo
13.
The Zoo
14.
The Zoo
15.
The Zoo
16.
The Zoo
17.
The Zoo
18.
The Zoo

Pattern Party

Objective: To reinforce the skill of creating shape patterns with 2 or more repetitions

Use with Kindergarten anytime after Chapter 2, Lesson 2-10; Grade 1, anytime after Chapter 1, Lesson 1-3.

You Will Need

Pattern Party game cards (40)

1 number cube

How to Start

Two Players

Each player receives 20 cards.

How to Play

Players use as many cards as possible to create patterns that are repeated at least 2 times (for example, square, circle, square, circle).

Each player places the cards faceup in rows showing the patterns. Players try to use as many of their cards as possible in the patterns.

Players check each other's patterns to see that they are correct.

Players may not add to each other's patterns.

The game ends when no more patterns can be made. The winner is the player with fewer cards left over after all patterns have been checked.

There is no answer key for Pattern Party.

Variation

Each player tosses the number cube. The player with the greater number is Player 1 and starts the game. Player 2 gives 6 cards to each player. The remaining cards are placed facedown in a pile.

Player 1 uses his or her 6 game cards to create a pattern that is repeated at least 2 times (for example, square, circle, square, circle). Player 1 places the cards faceup showing the pattern that was made. Player 2 checks to see the pattern is correct.

If Player 1 makes a correct pattern, he or she keeps the "extra" cards not used and draws from the pile the same number of cards used to make the pattern.

If the player cannot make a pattern, he or she draws 1 card from the pile. Player 1's turn ends and it is Player 2's turn.

During each player's turn, he or she can add cards onto the other player's patterns.

The game ends when there are no more cards in the pile. The winner is the player with the least number of "extra" cards.

1.

Pattern Party

2.

Pattern Party

3.

Pattern Party

4.

Pattern Party

5.

Pattern Party

6.

Pattern Party

7.

Pattern Party

8.

Pattern Party

9.

Pattern Party

10.

Pattern Party

11.

Pattern Party

12.

Pattern Party

13.

Pattern Party

14.

Pattern Party

15.

Pattern Party

16.

Pattern Party

17.

Pattern Party

18.

Pattern Party

19.

Pattern Party

20.

Pattern Party

21.

Pattern Party

22.

Pattern Party

23.

Pattern Party

24.

Pattern Party

25.

Pattern Party

26.

Pattern Party

27.

Pattern Party

28.

Pattern Party

29.

Pattern Party

30.

Pattern Party

31.

Pattern Party

32.

Pattern Party

33.

Pattern Party

34.

Pattern Party

35.

Pattern Party

36.

Pattern Party

37.

Pattern Party

38.

Pattern Party

39.

Pattern Party

40.

Pattern Party

Leap Frog

Objective: To reinforce the skill of comparing numbers through 10

Use with Kindergarten anytime after Chapter 4, Lesson 4-7; Grade 1, anytime after Chapter 1, Lesson 1-11.

You Will Need

Leap Frog game board
Leap Frog game cards (36)
Leap Frog answer key
or counters (20 for each player)
1 number cube
1 pawn for each player

How to Start

Two or Three Players

Each player tosses the number cube. The player who tosses the least number is Player 1 and starts the game.

Player 2 mixes the game cards and places them facedown on the green Card Pile on the game board.

Each player puts his or her pawn on the Start lilypad.

How to Play

Player 1 takes the top 2 cards from the green Card Pile, counts the number of objects on each card, and tells which is the greater number.

Player 2 can use counters to check Player 1's answer. If it is correct, Player 1 rolls the number cube and moves his or her pawn the same number of lily pads as the number shown on the cube.

If the answer is not correct, no move is made.

Then the cards are placed on the red Card Pile, and it is Player 2's turn.

Players take turns, with the player to the left going next. If a player lands on a lily pad occupied by another player, he or she may leap over that player to the next space.

The winner is the first person to leap out of the pond from the last lily pad onto Finish.

Answer Key: Leap Frog

1. 10	13. 4	25. 6
2. 10	14. 4	26. 5
3. 9	15. 3	27. 4
4. 9	16. 3	28. 3
5. 8	17. 2	29. 2
6. 8	18. 2	30. 1
7. 7	19. 1	31. 2
8. 7	20. 1	32. 3
9. 6	21. 10	33. 4
10. 6	22. 9	34. 5
11. 5	23. 8	35. 6
12. 5	24. 7	36. 7

Variation

Each player picks 2 cards, counts the number of objects on each card, and tells which is the lesser number.

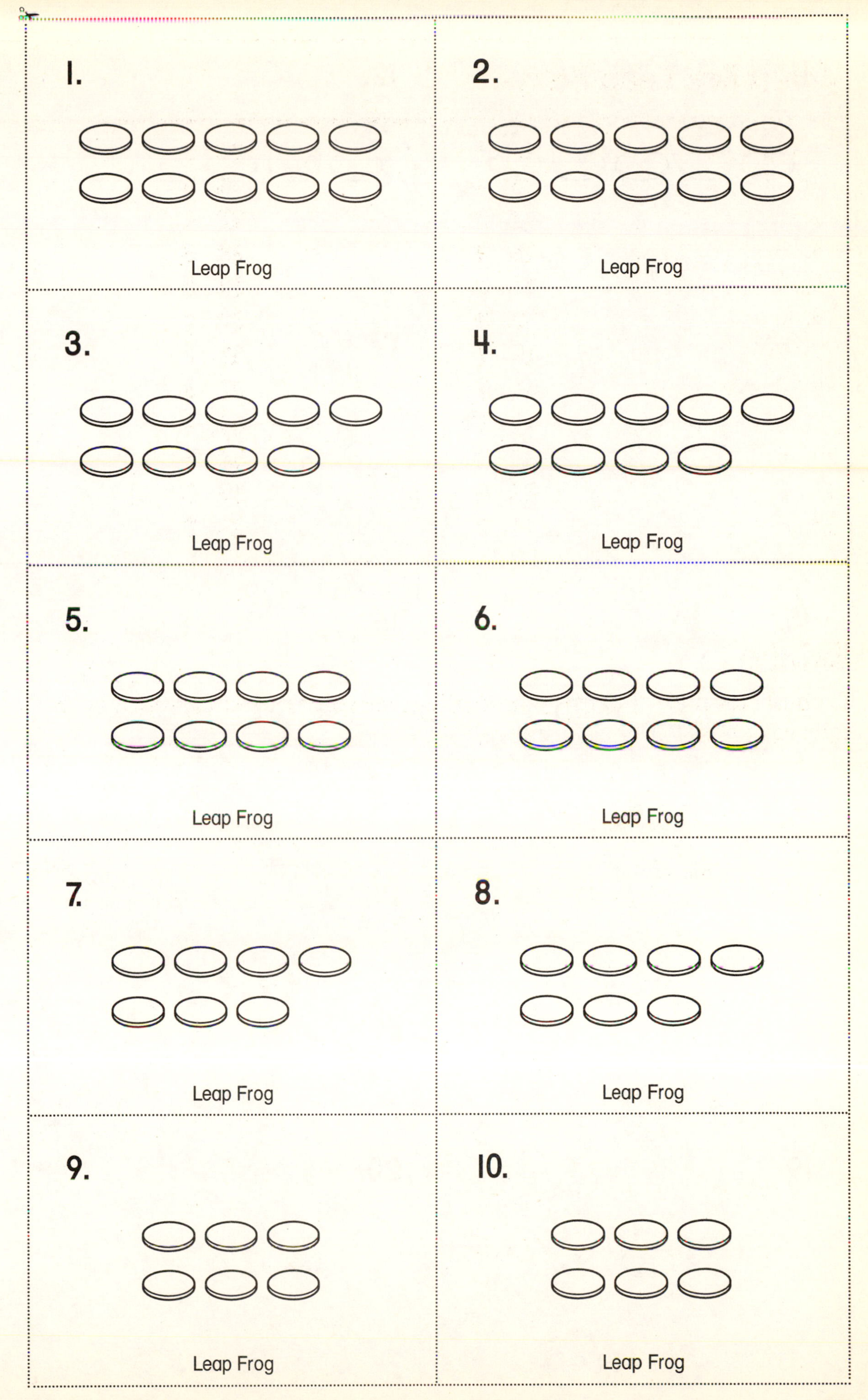
1.
Leap Frog
2.
Leap Frog
3.
Leap Frog
4.
Leap Frog
5.
Leap Frog
6.
Leap Frog
7.
Leap Frog
8.
Leap Frog
9.
Leap Frog
10.
Leap Frog

11.

Leap Frog

12.

Leap Frog

13.

Leap Frog

14.

Leap Frog

15.

Leap Frog

16.

Leap Frog

17.

Leap Frog

18.

Leap Frog

19.

Leap Frog

20.

Leap Frog

21.

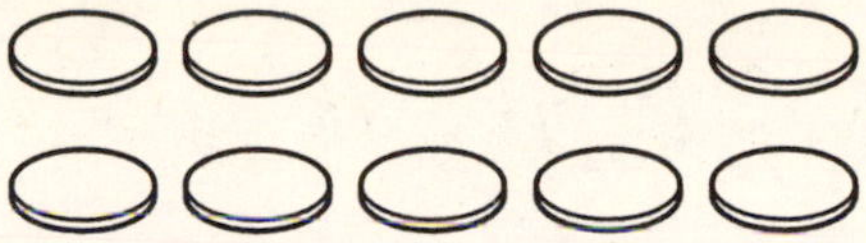

Leap Frog

22.

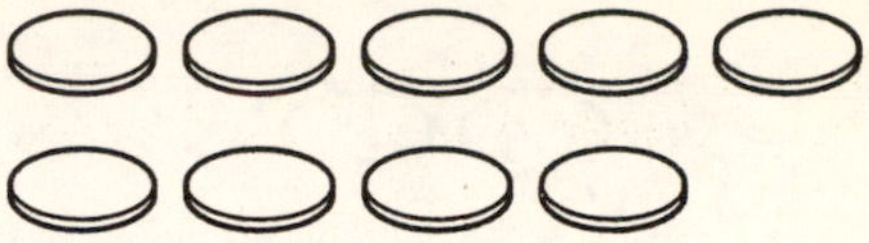

Leap Frog

23.

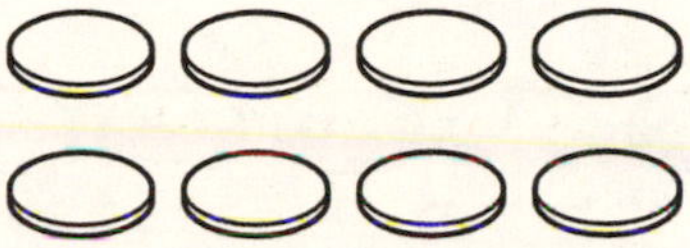

Leap Frog

24.

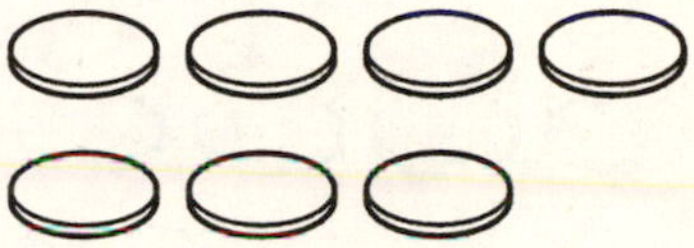

Leap Frog

25.

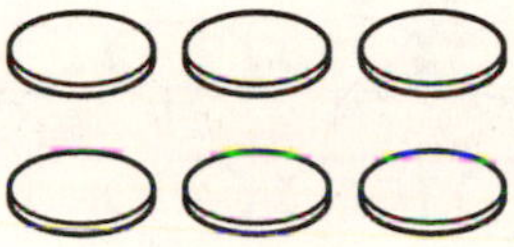

Leap Frog

26.

Leap Frog

27.

Leap Frog

28.

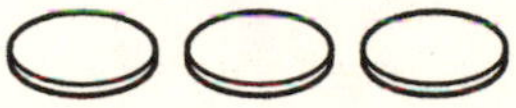

Leap Frog

29.

Leap Frog

30.

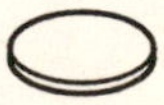

Leap Frog

31.

Leap Frog

32.

Leap Frog

33.

Leap Frog

34.

Leap Frog

35.

Leap Frog

36.

Leap Frog

Fewer and Fewer

Objective: To reinforce the skill of subtracting 1 or 2 to make new numbers

Use with Kindergarten anytime after Chapter 9, Lesson 9-7; Grade 1, anytime after Chapter 1, Lesson 1-10.

You Will Need

Fewer and Fewer game cards (32)
- Cards 1–16 are answer cards
- Cards 17–32 are question cards

Teacher's Note: You may want to use a different color for each set of game cards.

Fewer and Fewer answer key *or* counters (6 for each player)

1 number cube

How to Start

Two Players

Each player tosses the number cube. The player who tosses the greater number is Player 1 and starts the game.

Player 2 mixes the answer cards (1–16) and places them faceup in rows between the players. Then Player 2 mixes the question cards (17–32) and places them facedown in a card pile between the players.

How to Play

Fewer and Fewer is a matching game.

Player 1 takes the top question card from the card pile, counts all of the objects on the card, checks how many are crossed out with an X, and tells how many are left. Player 1 checks the answer cards to find a match. To make a match, the player finds a card with the number that tells how many objects are left.

If a match is made, Player 2 uses the answer key or counters to check Player 1's match. If it is correct, Player 1 picks up both cards and places the pair aside.

If it is not correct, the question card is placed facedown at the bottom of the card pile. Then it is Player 2's turn.

Players take turns.

The game ends when there are no question cards left in the pile. The winner is the player with more pairs.

Answer Key: Fewer and Fewer

Card	matches	Card
1.		17.
2.		18.
3.		19.
4.		20.
5.		21.
6.		22.
7.		23.
8.		24.
9.		25.
10.		26.
11.		27.
12.		28.
13.		29.
14.		30.
15.		31.
16.		32.

1. 3 Fewer and Fewer	2. 1 Fewer and Fewer
3. 2 Fewer and Fewer	4. 4 Fewer and Fewer
5. 4 Fewer and Fewer	6. 3 Fewer and Fewer
7. 2 Fewer and Fewer	8. 1 Fewer and Fewer
9. 5 Fewer and Fewer	10. 5 Fewer and Fewer

11. 2 Fewer and Fewer	12. 4 Fewer and Fewer
13. 5 Fewer and Fewer	14. 3 Fewer and Fewer
15. 2 Fewer and Fewer	16. 4 Fewer and Fewer
17. Fewer and Fewer	18. Fewer and Fewer
19. Fewer and Fewer	20. Fewer and Fewer

21.

Fewer and Fewer

22.

Fewer and Fewer

23.

Fewer and Fewer

24.

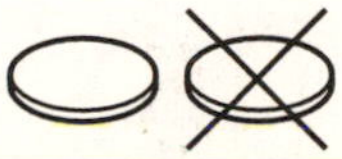

Fewer and Fewer

25.

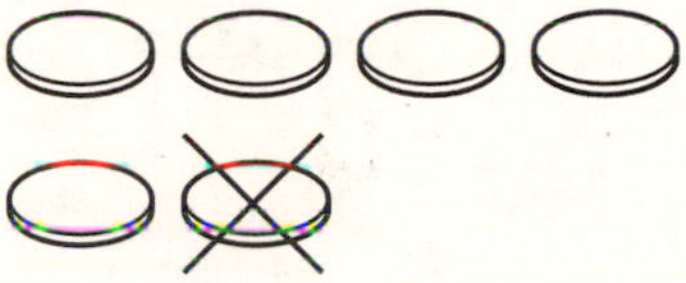

Fewer and Fewer

26.

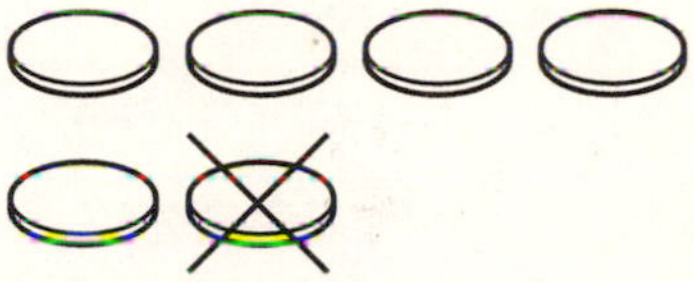

Fewer and Fewer

27.

Fewer and Fewer

28.

Fewer and Fewer

29.

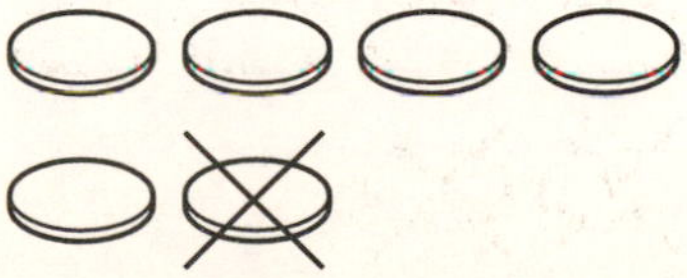

Fewer and Fewer

30.

Fewer and Fewer

31.

Fewer and Fewer

32.

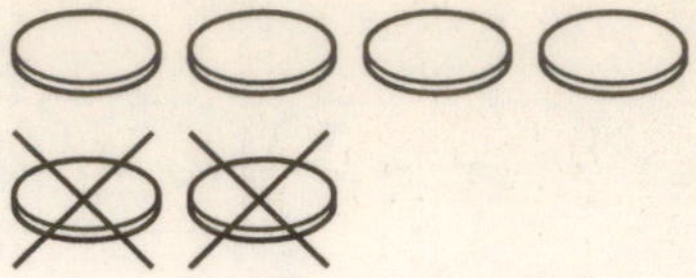

Fewer and Fewer

Prehistoric Animals

Objective: To reinforce the skill of sequencing numbers through 31

Use with Kindergarten anytime after Chapter 5, Lesson 5-7; Grade 1, anytime after Chapter 7, Lesson 7-3; Grade 2, anytime after Chapter 3, Lesson 3-7.

You Will Need

Prehistoric Animals game board

Prehistoric Animals game cards (18)

Teacher's Note: You will need to cut on the dotted cut lines, fold on the solid fold lines, and paste the front and back sides of the cards together for this game.

Prehistoric Animals answer key *or* counters (31 for each player)

1 number cube

How to Start

Two Players

Each player tosses the number cube. The player who tosses the lesser number is Player 1 and starts the game.

Player 2 mixes the game cards and places them facedown in a card pile on the green rectangle on the game board.

How to Play

Player 1 takes the top card from the card pile and gives the next number in order.

Player 2 uses the answer key or counters to see if Player 1's answer is correct. If it is correct, Player 1 places the card on the same answer on the game board with the picture side up. If it is not correct, the card is placed at the bottom of the card pile. Then it is Player 2's turn.

Players take turns.

The winner is the player who puts the last card on the game board to complete the picture.

Answer Key: Prehistoric Animals

1. 16	7. 21	13. 12
2. 9	8. 31	14. 17
3. 3	9. 24	15. 20
4. 14	10. 28	16. 30
5. 11	11. 7	17. 23
6. 18	12. 6	18. 15

Variation

One player can practice writing groups of numerals in sequential order on the board. The other player writes the two numbers that come before and after the written series produced by the first player.

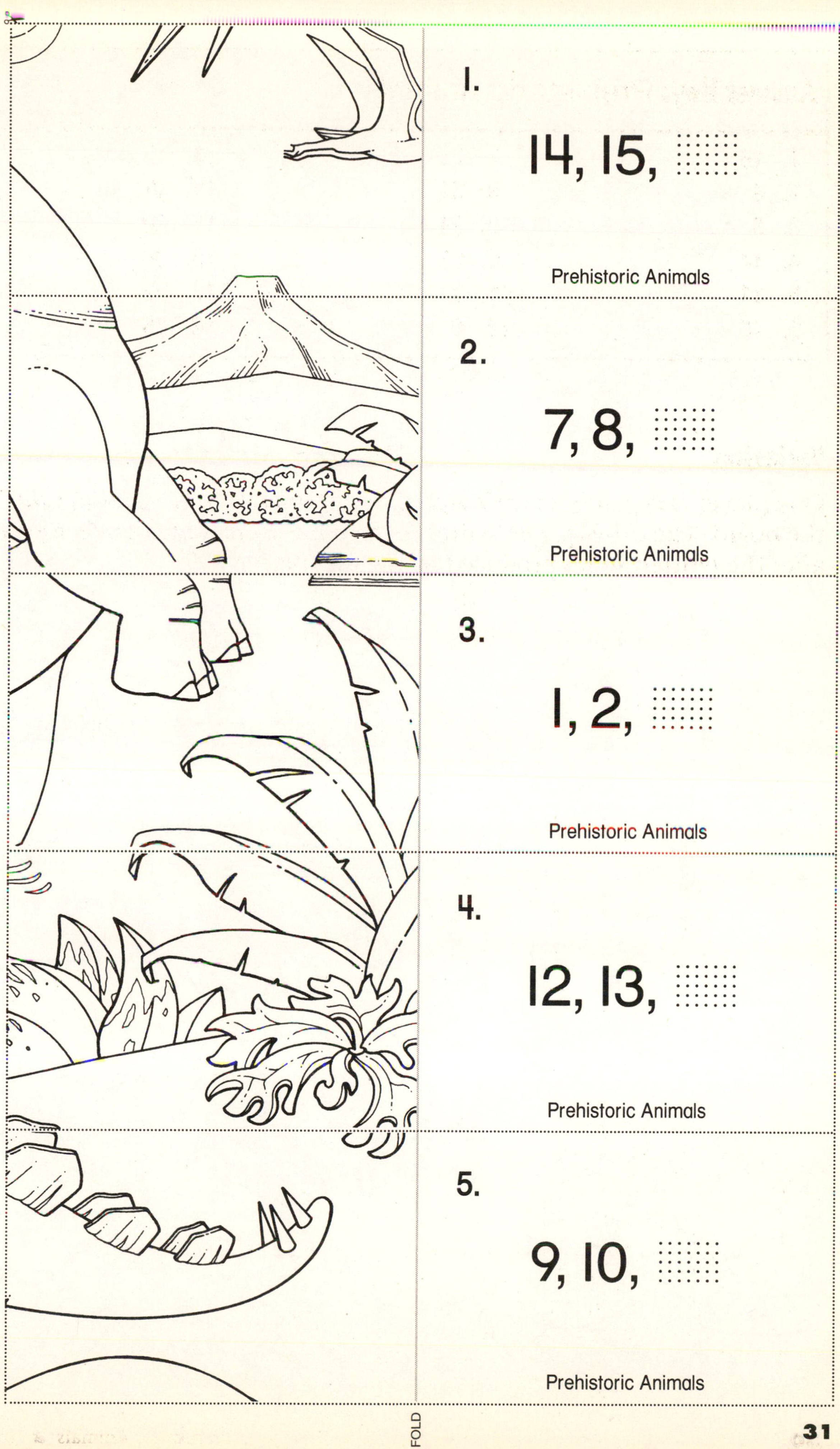
1.
14, 15,
Prehistoric Animals
2.
7, 8,
Prehistoric Animals
3.
1, 2,
Prehistoric Animals
4.
12, 13,
Prehistoric Animals
5.
9, 10,
Prehistoric Animals
FOLD

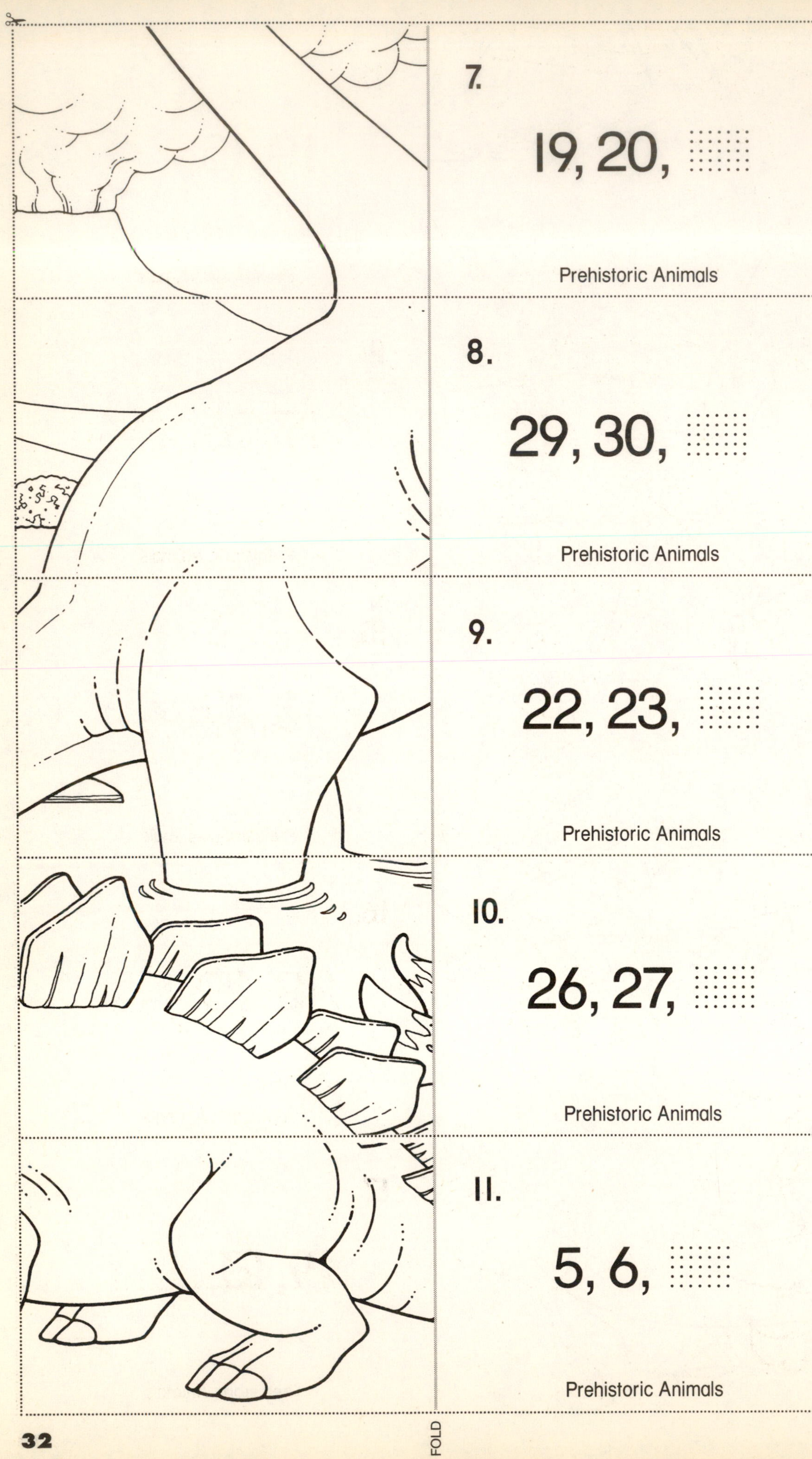

7.

19, 20, ⬚

Prehistoric Animals

8.

29, 30, ⬚

Prehistoric Animals

9.

22, 23, ⬚

Prehistoric Animals

10.

26, 27, ⬚

Prehistoric Animals

11.

5, 6, ⬚

Prehistoric Animals

FOLD

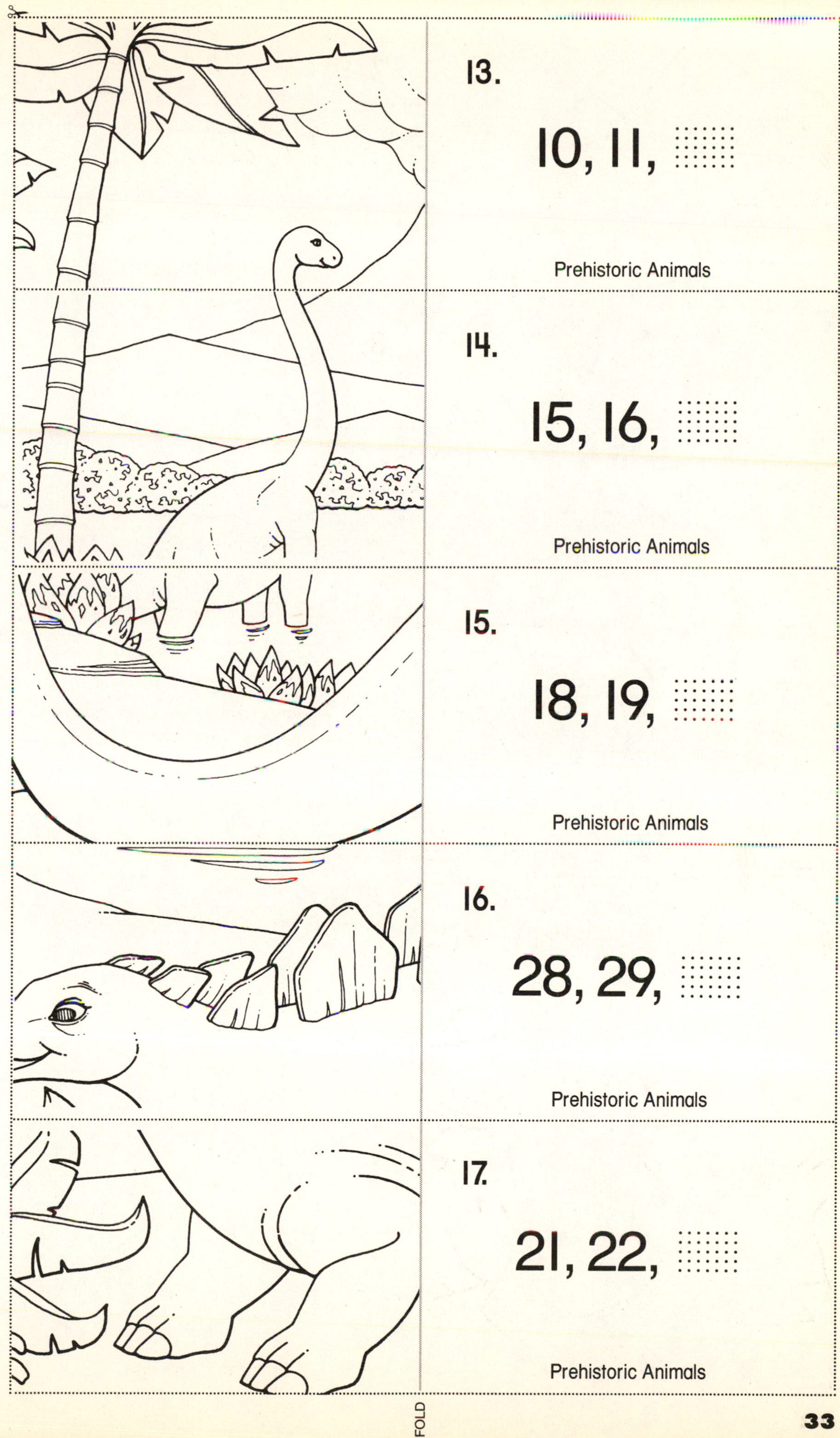
13.
10, 11,
Prehistoric Animals
14.
15, 16,
Prehistoric Animals
15.
18, 19,
Prehistoric Animals
16.
28, 29,
Prehistoric Animals
17.
21, 22,
Prehistoric Animals
FOLD

6.

16, 17, ____

Prehistoric Animals

12.

4, 5, ____

Prehistoric Animals

18.

13, 14, ____

Prehistoric Animals

FOLD

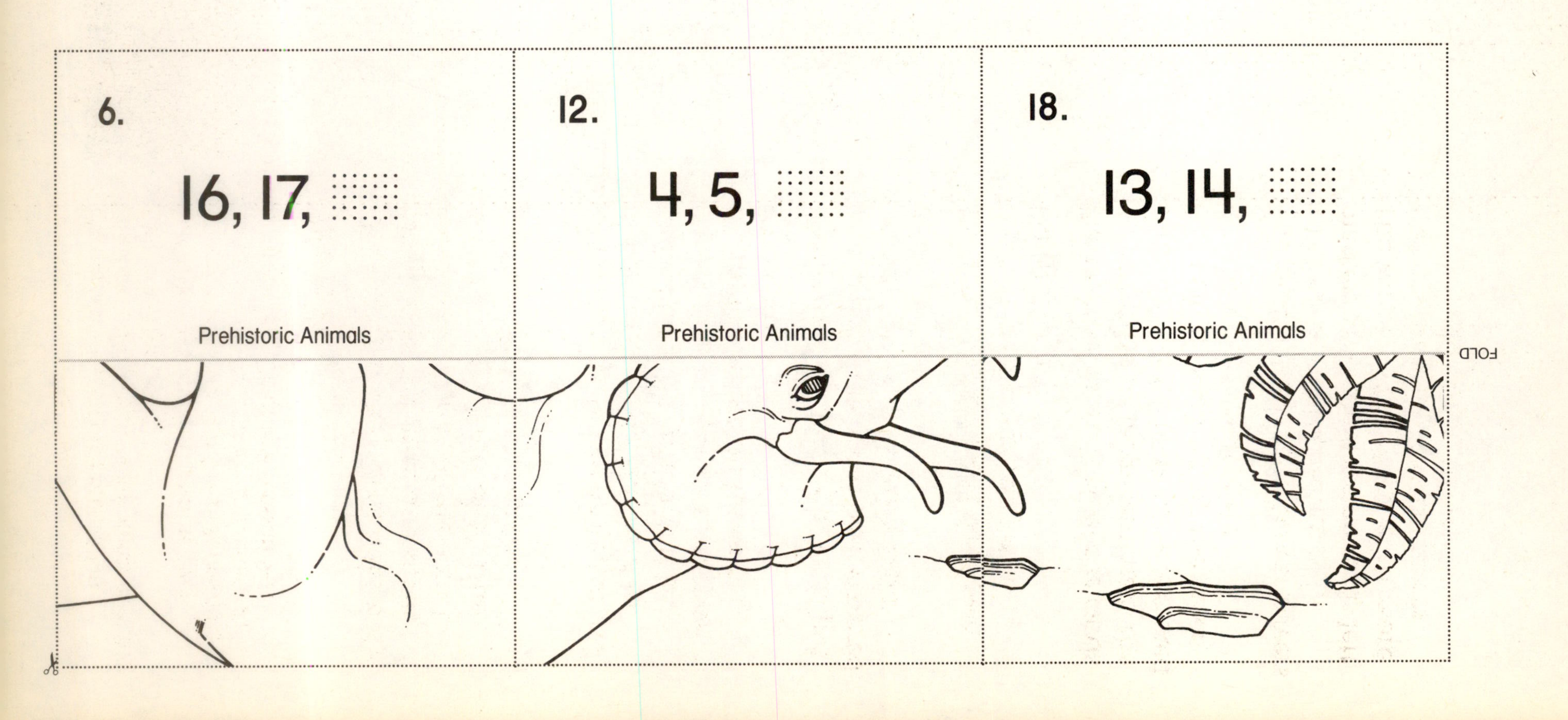

Inchworm

Objective: To reinforce the skill of measuring the length of an object by using arbitrary units

Use with Kindergarten anytime after Chapter 6, Lesson 6-5; Grade 1, anytime after Chapter 10, Lesson 10-1; Grade 2, anytime after Chapter 9, Lesson 9-1.

You Will Need

Inchworm game board
Inchworm game cards (36)
Inchworm Units of Measure cards (2)
Inchworm answer key *or* Inchworm Units of Measure card
1 number cube
20 round markers in 2 colors (10 of each color)

How to Start

Two Players

Each player tosses the number cube. The player who tosses the lesser number is Player 1 and starts the game.

Player 2 mixes the game cards (not including the Units of Measure cards) and places them facedown in a card pile on the green rectangle on the game board.

Each player starts with 10 round markers of 1 color.

Players use Units of Measure cards to find the measurements.

How to Play

Player 1 takes the top card from the card pile on the green rectangle, measures the units of the object with his or her Units of Measure card, and tells how long the object is.

Player 2 uses the answer key or his or her Units of Measure card to check Player 1's answer. If it is correct, Player 1 puts a marker on the same number on his or her inchworm.

If it is not correct, no marker is put down. If it already has been covered or is not there, no marker is put down.

Then the card is placed facedown on the red rectangle, and it is Player 2's turn.

Players take turns. If all of the cards on the green rectangle are used, the cards on the red rectangle are mixed and placed facedown on the green rectangle to be used again.

The game ends when a player covers all of his or her inchworm with markers, or if there are no cards left. The winner is the player with more markers on his or her inchworm.

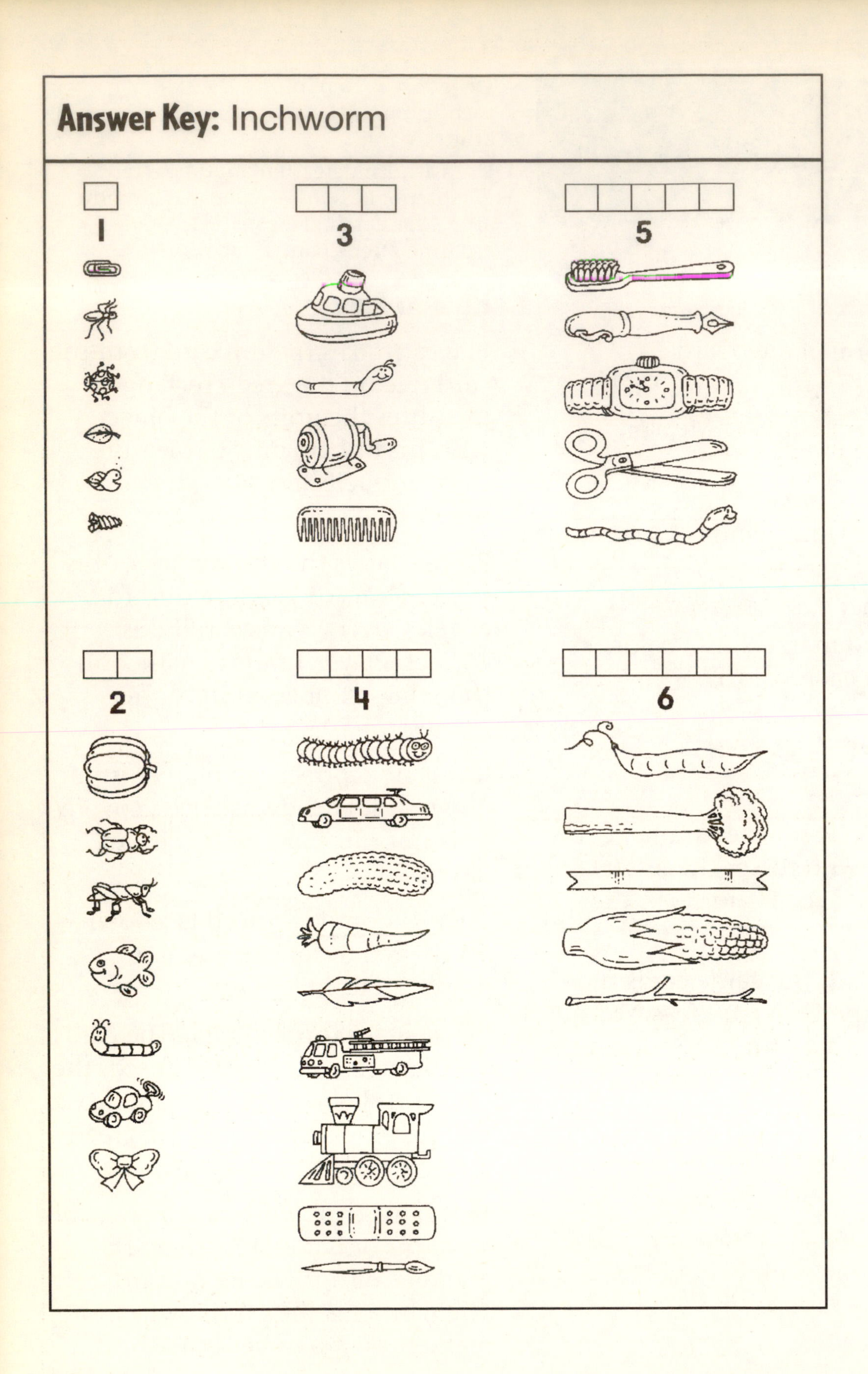

Variation

Players take turns taking two cards at a time from the card pile. Players count the units on both cards and tell which object is longer.

Inchworm

Inchworm

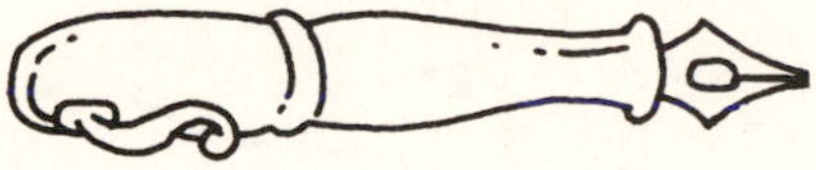

Inchworm

Inchworm

Inchworm

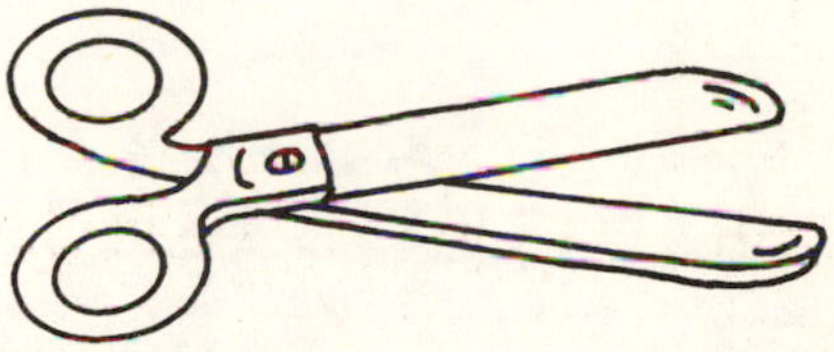

Inchworm

Inchworm

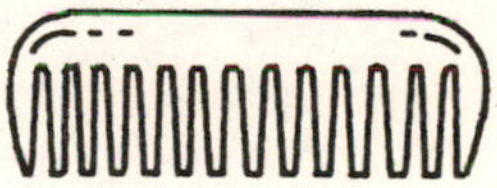

Inchworm

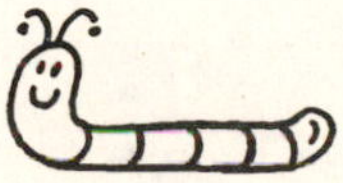

Inchworm

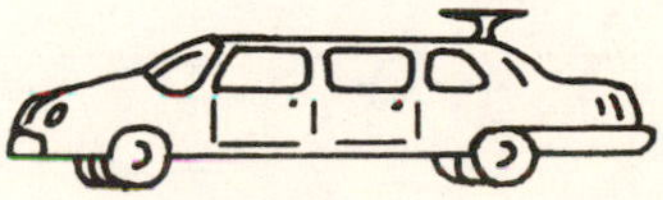

Inchworm

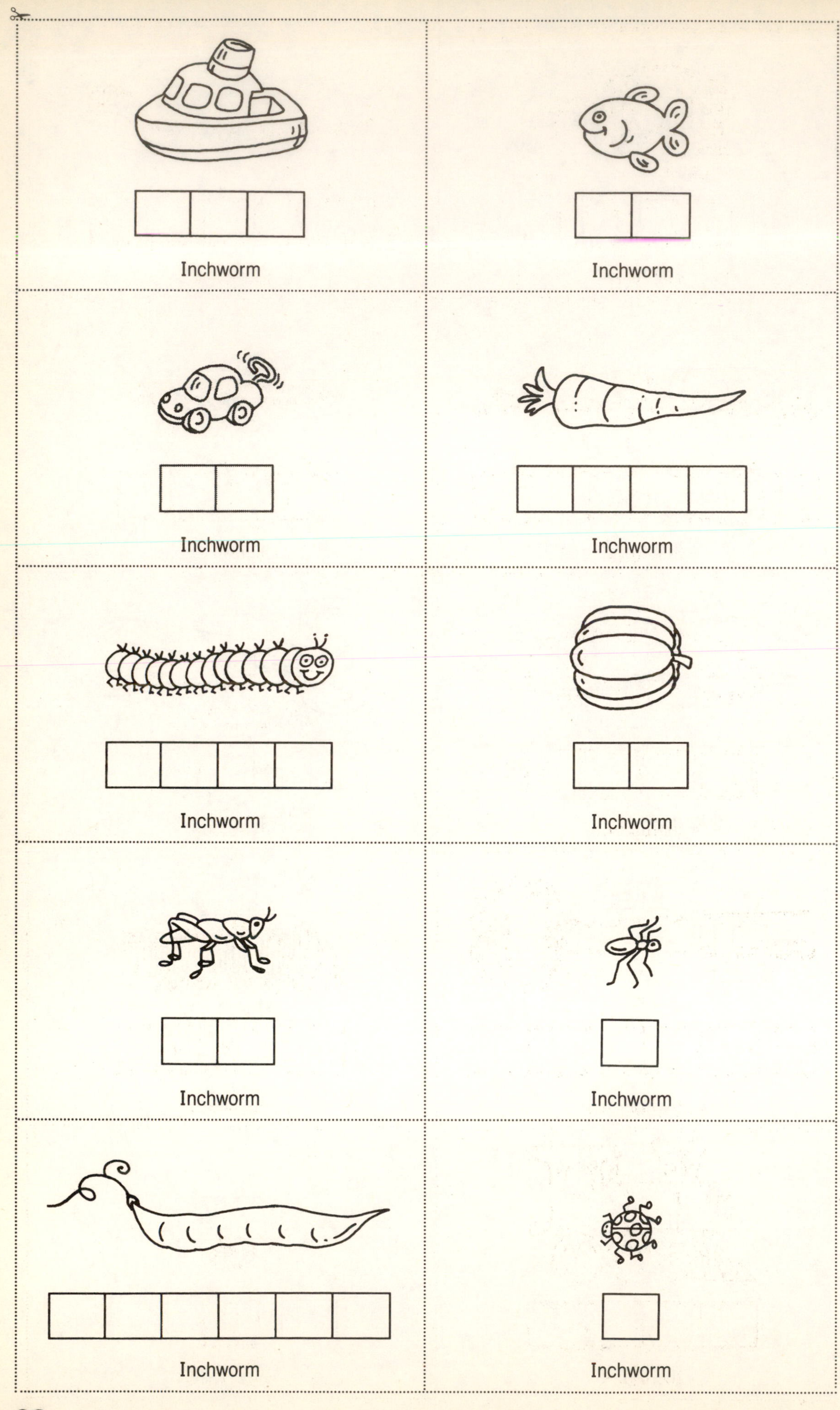
Inchworm
Inchworm
Inchworm
Inchworm
Inchworm
Inchworm
Inchworm
Inchworm
Inchworm
Inchworm

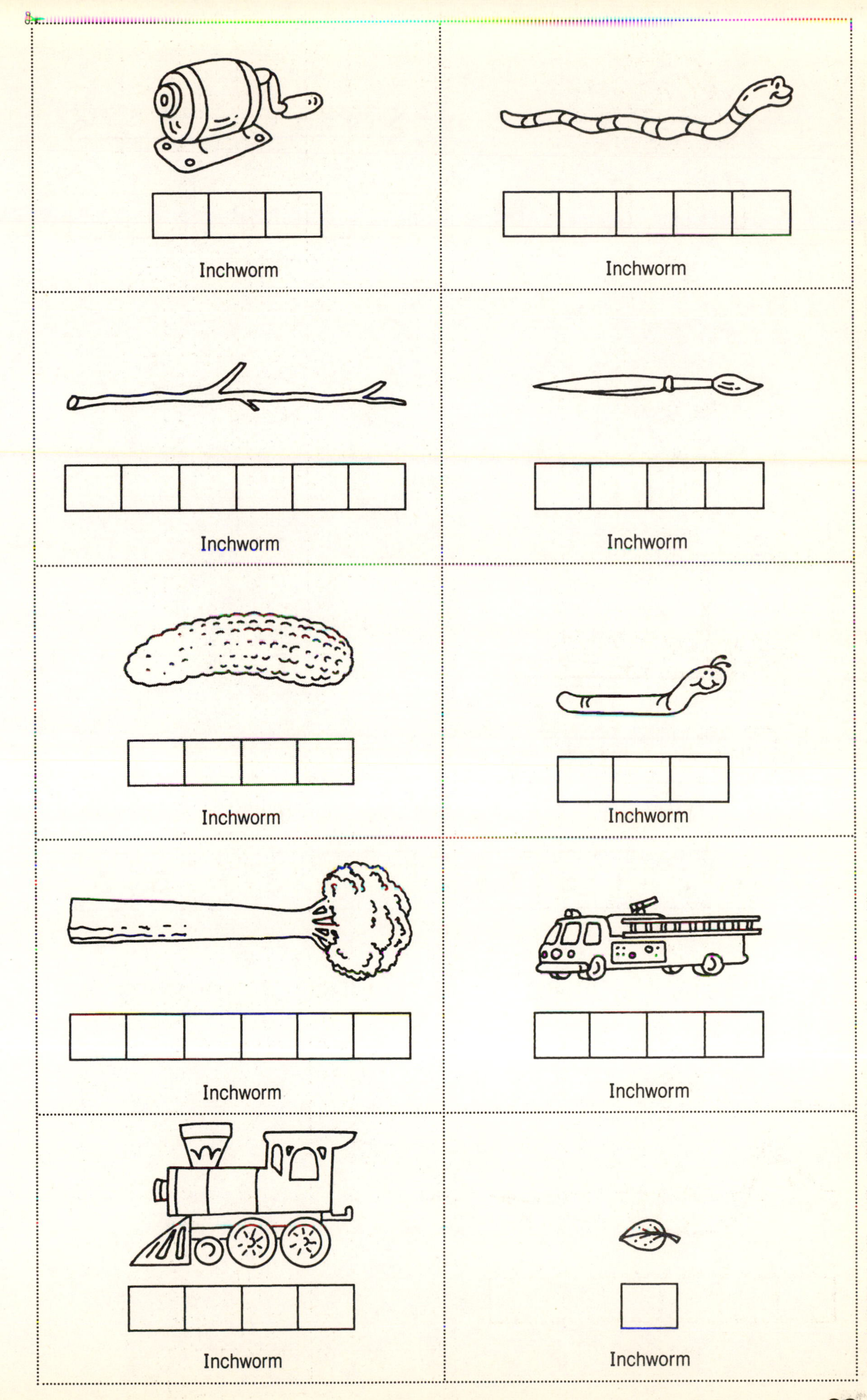
Inchworm
Inchworm
Inchworm
Inchworm
Inchworm
Inchworm
Inchworm
Inchworm
Inchworm
Inchworm

Inchworm

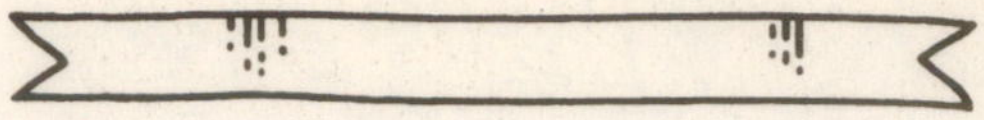

Inchworm

Inchworm

Inchworm

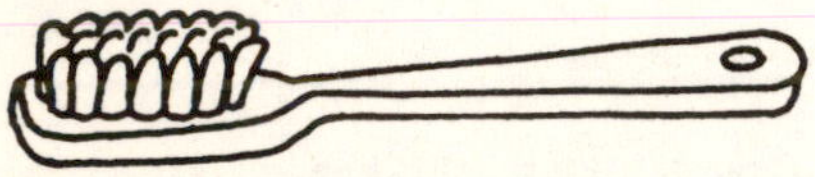

Inchworm

Inchworm

1	2	3	4	5	6

Units of Measure

Inchworm

1	2	3	4	5	6

Units of Measure

Inchworm

The Farm

Objective: To reinforce the skill of using standard clocks to tell time to the hour

Use with Kindergarten anytime after Chapter 7, Lesson 7-7; Grade 1, anytime after Chapter 6, Lesson 6-3; Grade 2, anytime after Chapter 8, Lesson 8-1.

You Will Need

The Farm game board

The Farm game cards (18)

Teacher's Note: You will need to cut on the dotted cut lines, fold on the solid fold lines, and paste the front and back sides of the cards together for this game.

The Farm answer key

1 number cube

How to Start

Two Players

Each player tosses the number cube. The player who tosses the lesser number is Player 1 and starts the game.

Player 2 mixes the game cards and places them facedown in a card pile on the green rectangle on the game board.

How to Play

Player 1 takes the top card from the card pile, and tells the time shown on the clock.

Player 2 uses the answer key to check if Player 1's answer is correct. If it is correct, the card is placed on the same answer on the farm grid with the picture side up.

If it is not correct, the card is placed facedown at the bottom of the card pile. Then it is Player 2's turn.

Players take turns.

The winner is the player who puts the last game card on the farm grid to complete the picture.

Answer Key: The Farm

1. 7 o'clock

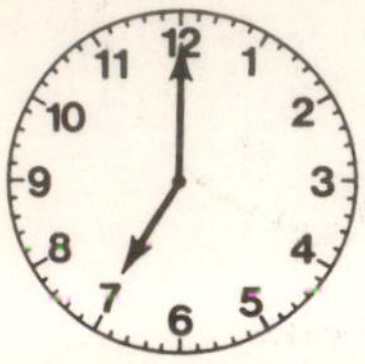

2. 3 o'clock

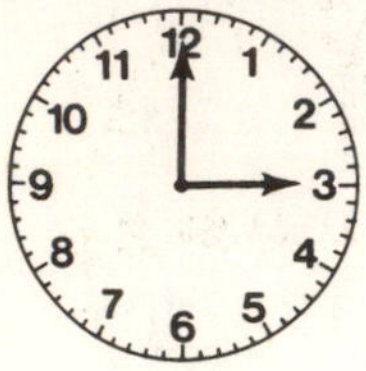

3. 4:00

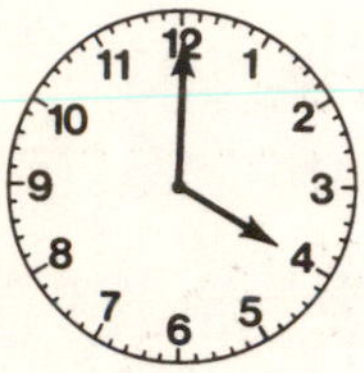

4. 6 o'clock

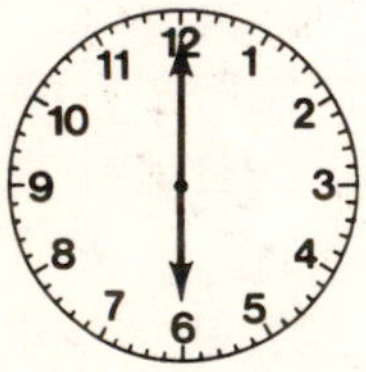

5. 2:00

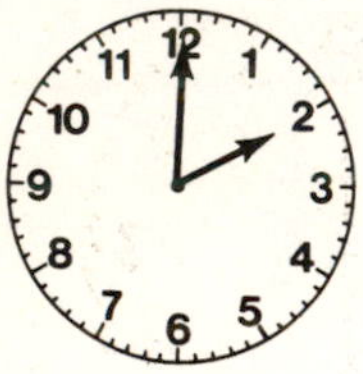

6. 6:00

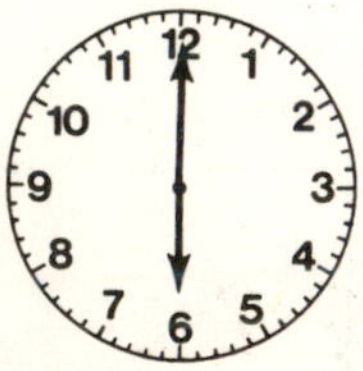

7. 5:00

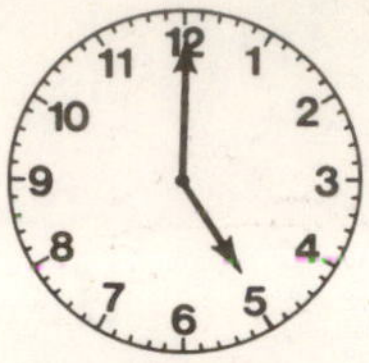

8. 12:00

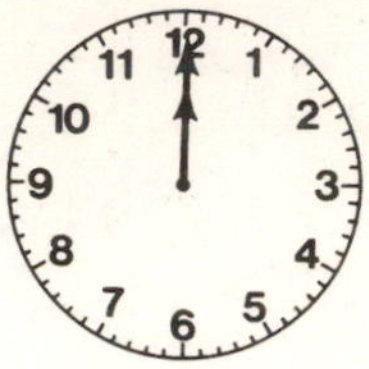

9. 1 o'clock

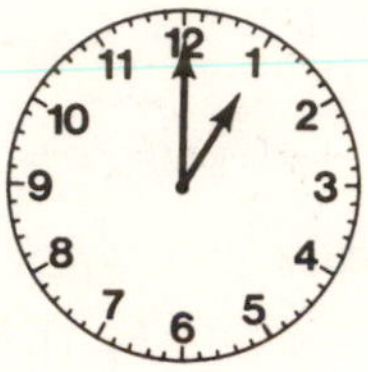

10. 10:00

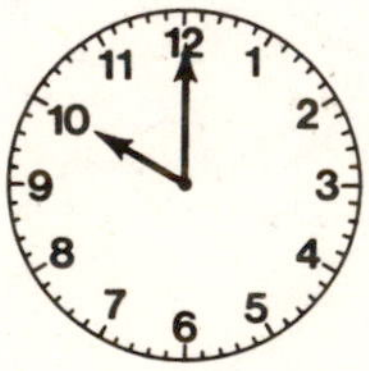

11. 11:00

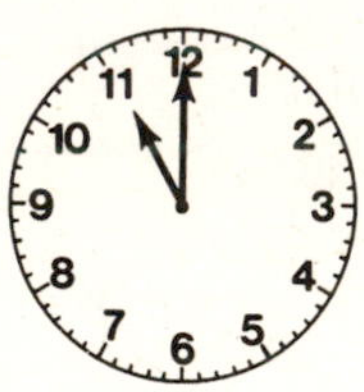

12. 9 o'clock

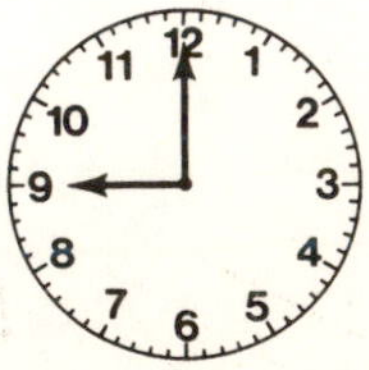

13. 8:00

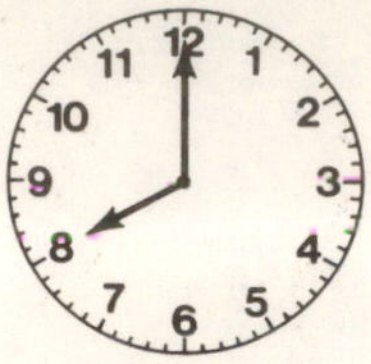

14. 9:00

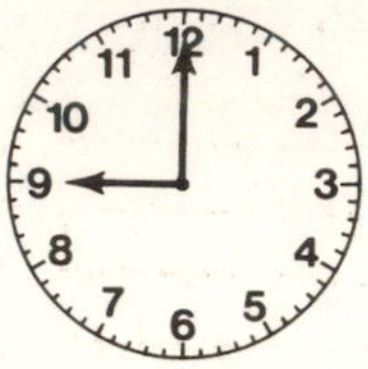

15. 4 o'clock

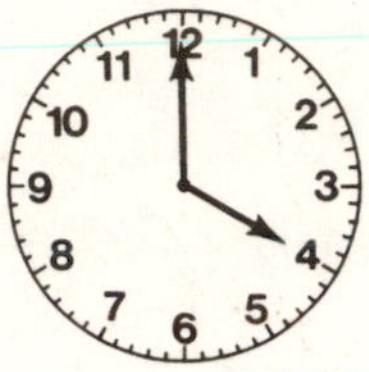

16. 1:00

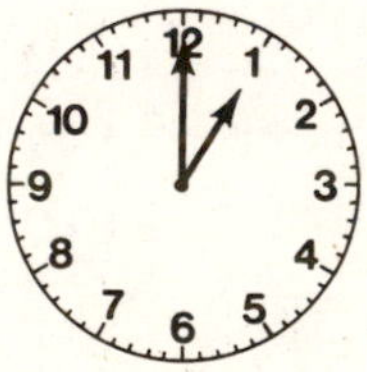

17. 7:00

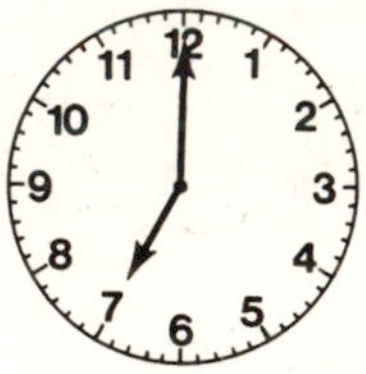

18. 3:00

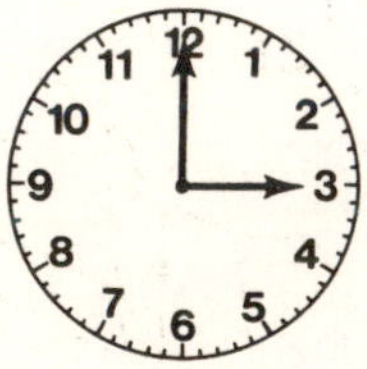

Variation

Player 1 takes the top card from the card pile and says the time on the clock. Player 2 then writes out the time on a piece of paper. Players can use the answer key to check the answers.

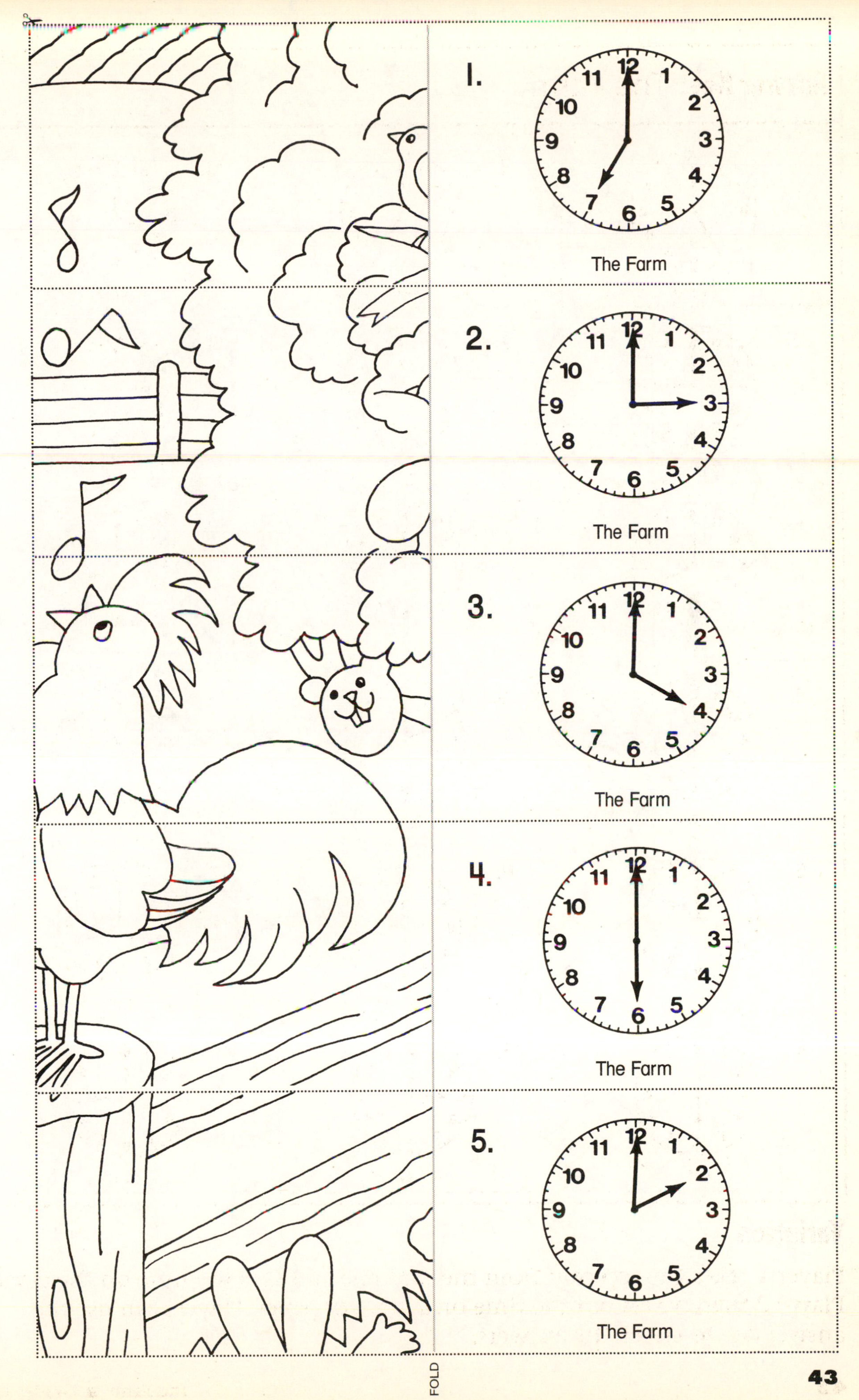
1.
The Farm
2.
The Farm
3.
The Farm
4.
The Farm
5.
The Farm
FOLD

7.

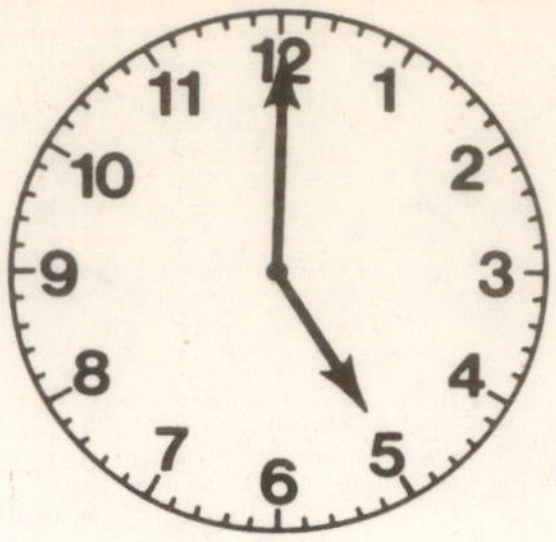

The Farm

8.

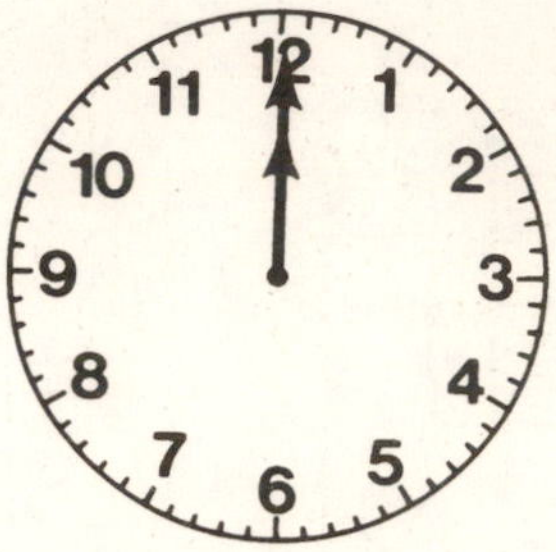

The Farm

9.

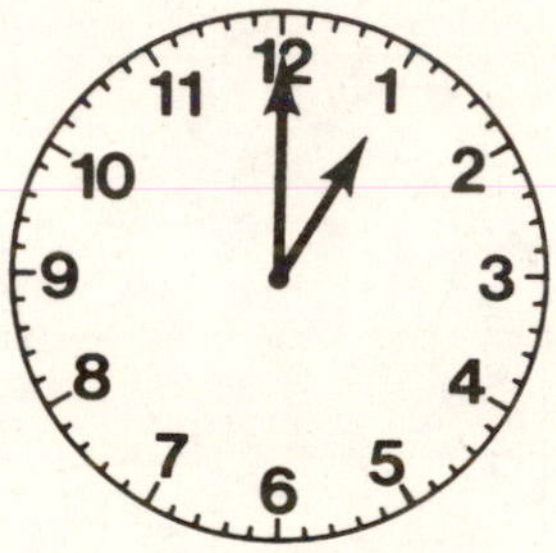

The Farm

10.

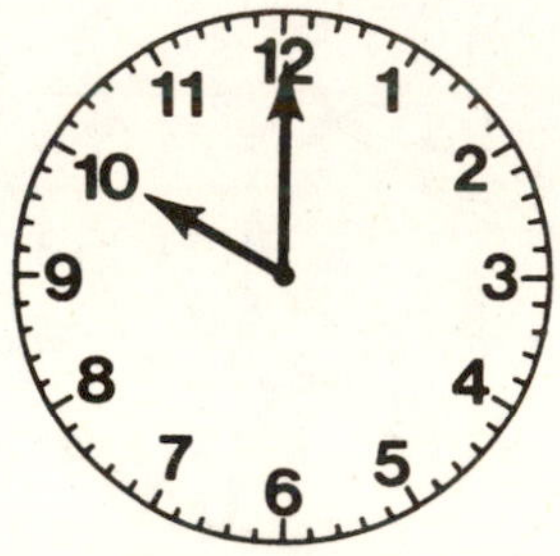

The Farm

11.

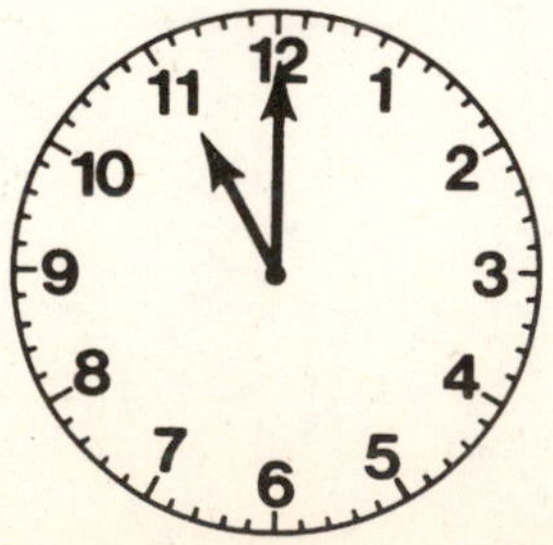

The Farm

FOLD

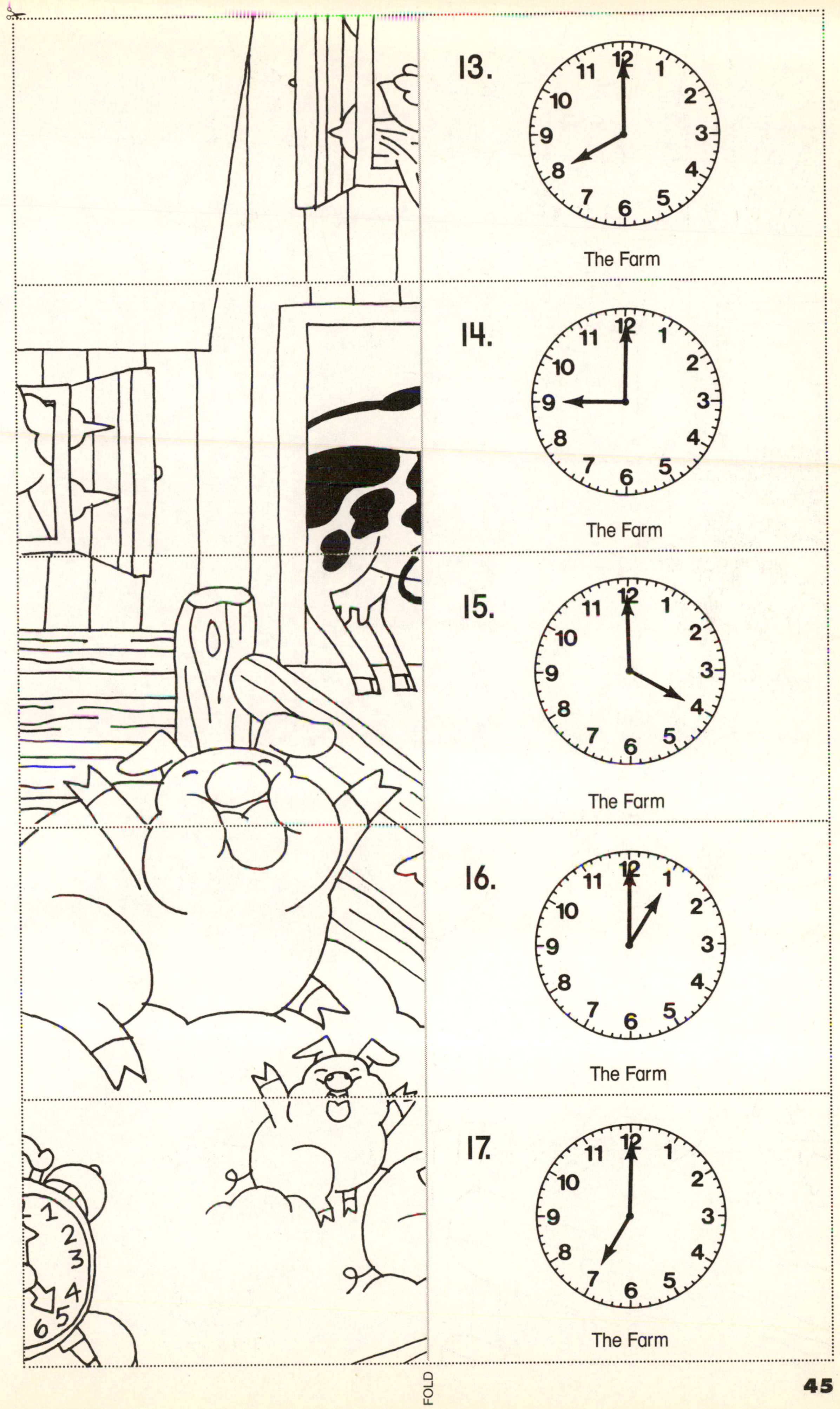
13.
The Farm
14.
The Farm
15.
The Farm
16.
The Farm
17.
The Farm
FOLD

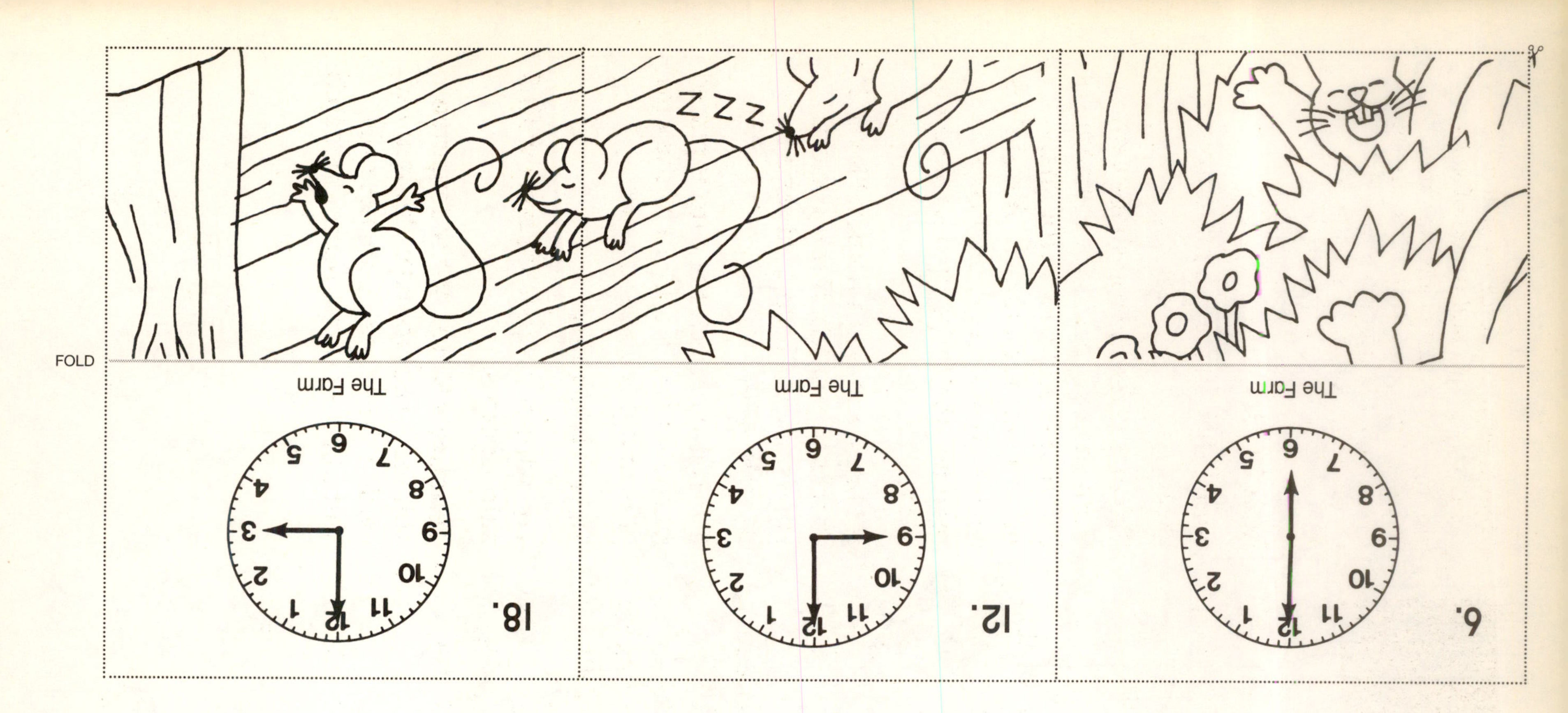
6.
The Farm
12.
The Farm
18.
The Farm
FOLD

Name That Shape

Objective: To reinforce the skill of identifying shapes and names of shapes

Use with Kindergarten anytime after Chapter 8, Lesson 8-5; Grade 1, anytime after Chapter 5, Lesson 5-4; Grade 2, anytime after Chapter 7, Lesson 7-2.

You Will Need

Name That Shape game cards (36)
- Cards 1–18 are shape name cards
- Cards 19–36 are shape cards
- **Teacher's Note:** You may want to use a different color for each set of game cards.

1 number cube

How to Start

Two Players

Each player tosses the number cube. The player who tosses the lesser number is Player 1.

Player 2 mixes the shape name cards (1–18) and places them faceup in rows between the players. Then Player 2 mixes the shape cards (19–36) and places them facedown in a card pile between the players.

How to Play

Name that Shape is a matching game.

Player 1 takes the top shape card from the card pile, says the name of the shape, and checks the shape name cards for a match. A match is made when a shape on a card matches the shape on a shape name card.

If Player 1 makes a match, Player 2 checks the match. If it is correct, Player 1 keeps both cards and puts the pair aside.

If it is not correct, the card is placed facedown at the bottom of the card pile, and it is Player 2's turn.

Players take turns.

The winner is the first player with 5 pairs of cards.

Teacher's Note: At Kindergarten, you may want to have children use cards 1–36 to match shapes only and not read shape names to match.

There is no answer key for Name That Shape.

Variation

Each set of cards is placed in a separate pile. Each player takes 3 cards from the shape name card pile and places them faceup in front of himself or herself. Player 1 takes the top card from the shape card pile, says the name of the shape, and checks to see if it matches any of the shapes on the cards in front of himself or herself. If a match is made, the card in front of the player must be replaced with a card from the shape name card pile.

1. circle

Name That Shape

2. cone

Name That Shape

3. cylinder

Name That Shape

4. square

Name That Shape

5. sphere

Name That Shape

6. square

Name That Shape

7. rectangle

Name That Shape

8. cube

Name That Shape

9. triangle

Name That Shape

10. cube

Name That Shape

11.

rectangle

Name That Shape

12.

sphere

Name That Shape

13.

square

Name That Shape

14.

cone

Name That Shape

15.

circle

Name That Shape

16.

square

Name That Shape

17.

cylinder

Name That Shape

18.

rectangle

Name That Shape

19.

Name That Shape

20.

Name That Shape

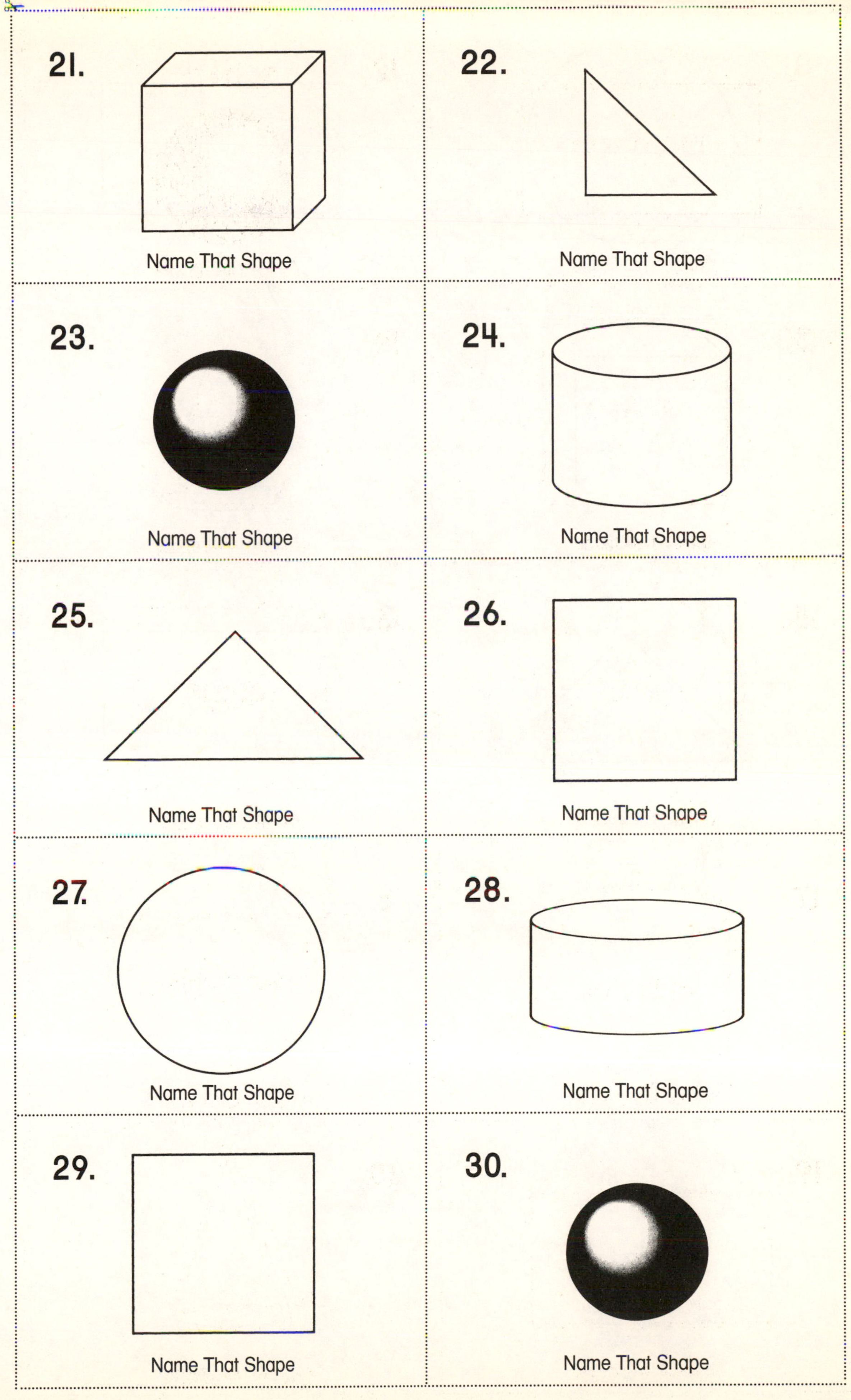
21.
Name That Shape
22.
Name That Shape
23.
Name That Shape
24.
Name That Shape
25.
Name That Shape
26.
Name That Shape
27.
Name That Shape
28.
Name That Shape
29.
Name That Shape
30.
Name That Shape

31.

Name That Shape

32.

Name That Shape

33.

Name That Shape

34.

Name That Shape

35.

Name That Shape

36.

Name That Shape

Sky-High

Objective: To reinforce the skill of finding sums by adding 0, 1, 2, or 3 to a given number

Use with Kindergarten anytime after Chapter 10, Lesson 10-6; Grade 1, anytime after Chapter 3, Lesson 3-3; Grade 2, anytime after Chapter 2, Lesson 2-1.

You Will Need

Sky-High game board

Sky-High game cards (18)

Teacher's Note: You will need to cut on the dotted cut lines, fold on the solid fold lines, and paste the front and back sides of the cards together for this game.

Sky High answer key
or counters (10 for each player)

1 number cube

How to Start

Two Players

Each player tosses the number cube. The player who tosses the greater number is Player 1 and starts the game.

Player 2 mixes the game cards and places them in a card pile facedown on the green Card Pile on the game board.

How to Play

Player 1 takes the top card from the green Card Pile, adds the numbers, and gives the answer.

Player 2 uses the answer key or counters to check Player 1's answer. If it is correct, Player 1 places the card on the same problem on the game board with the picture side up.

If the answer is not correct, the card is placed at the bottom of the card pile, and it is Player 2's turn.

Players take turns.

The winner is the player who puts the last card on the sky grid to complete the picture.

Answer Key: Sky-High

1. 7	7. 5	13. 9
2. 6	8. 3	14. 7
3. 7	9. 4	15. 6
4. 6	10. 10	16. 4
5. 4	11. 9	17. 8
6. 10	12. 8	18. 5

Variation

This game may be played by one player as an independent activity. The player takes a card, solves the problem, checks the answer, and puts the picture together.

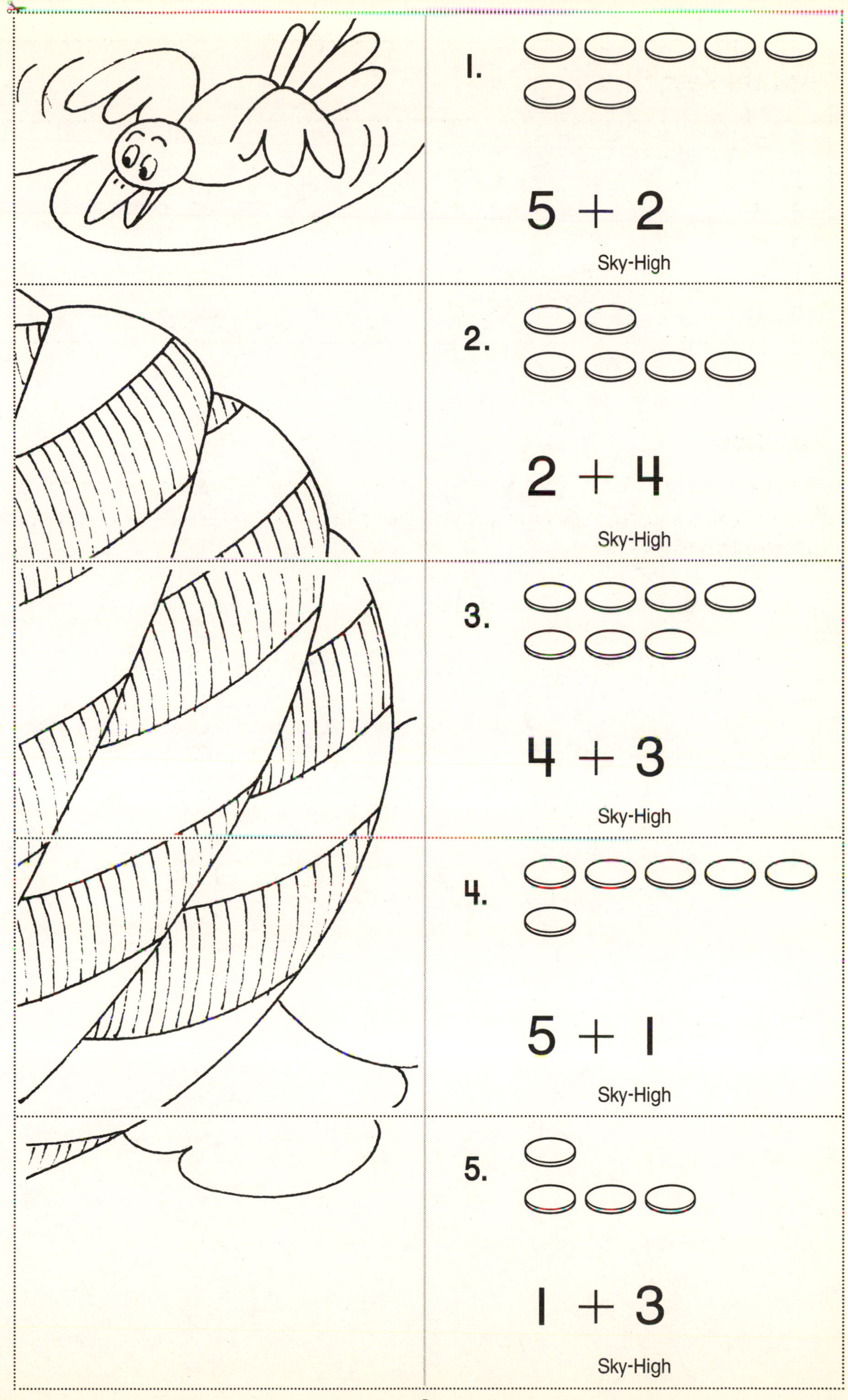
1.
5 + 2
Sky-High
2.
2 + 4
Sky-High
3.
4 + 3
Sky-High
4.
5 + 1
Sky-High
5.
1 + 3
Sky-High

FOLD

7.

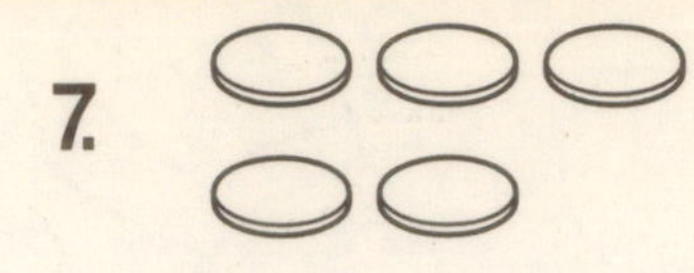

3 + 2

Sky-High

8.

2 + 1

Sky-High

9.

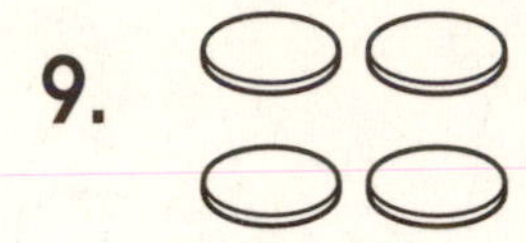

2 + 2

Sky-High

10.

8 + 2

Sky-High

11.

3 + 6

Sky-High

FOLD

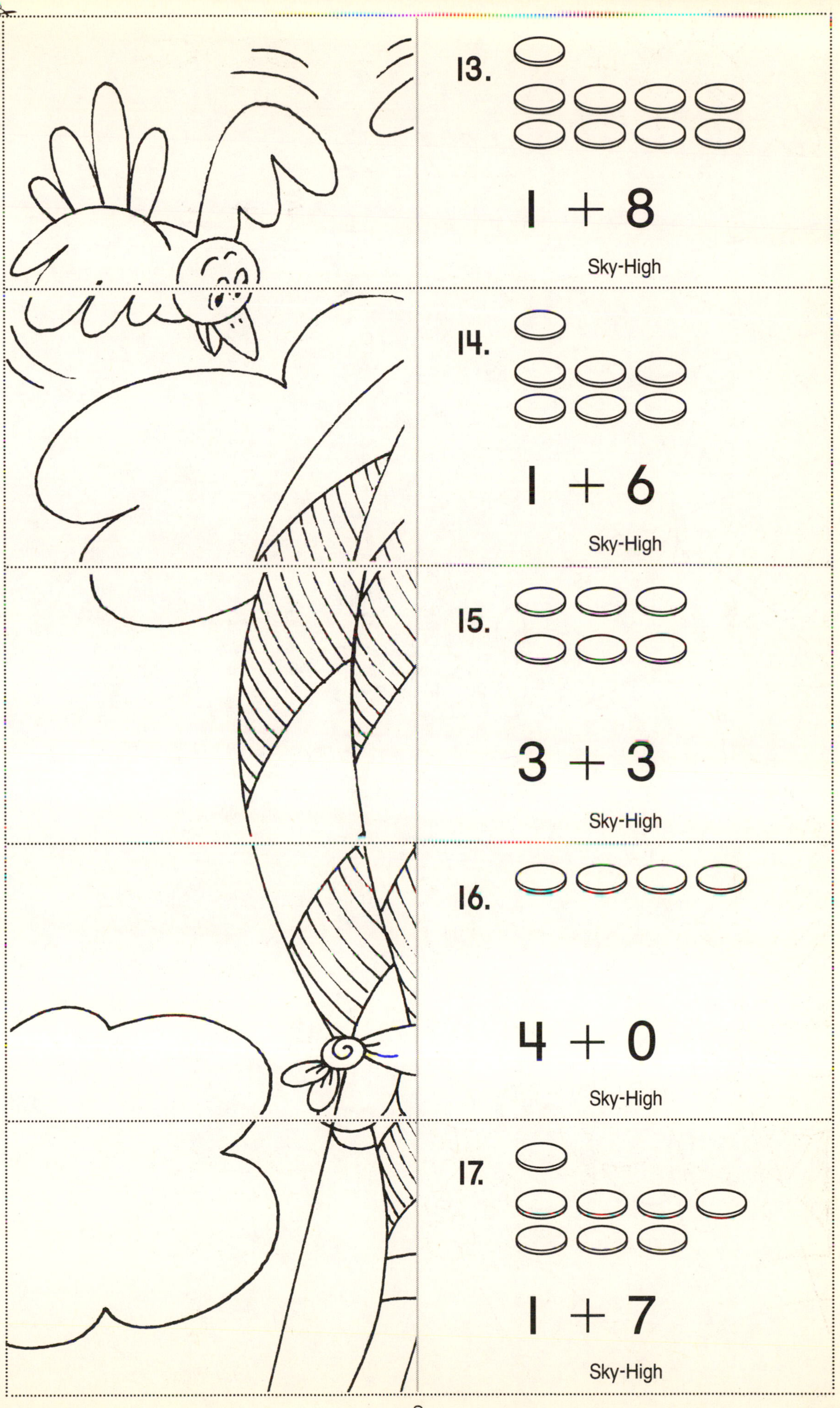
13.
1 + 8
Sky-High
14.
1 + 6
Sky-High
15.
3 + 3
Sky-High
16.
4 + 0
Sky-High
17.
1 + 7
Sky-High
FOLD

FOLD

6.

$3 + 7$

Sky-High

12.

$2 + 6$

Sky-High

18.

$2 + 3$

Sky-High

Bubble Mania

Objective: To reinforce the skill of subtracting from 10 or less

Use with Kindergarten anytime after Chapter 11, Lesson 11-6; Grade 1, anytime after Chapter 4, Lesson 4-6; Grade 2, anytime after Chapter 2, Lesson 2-8.

You Will Need

- Bubble Mania game board
- Bubble Mania game cards (36)
- Bubble Mania answer key *or* counters (10 for each player)
- 1 number cube
- 20 round markers in 2 colors (10 of each color)

How to Start

Two Players

Each player tosses the number cube. The player who tosses the greater number is Player 1 and starts the game.

Player 2 mixes the game cards and places them facedown on the green Card Pile on the gameboard.

Each player starts with 10 round markers of 1 color.

How to Play

Player 1 takes the top card from the green Card Pile, subtracts the numbers, reads the number sentence aloud and gives the answer.

Player 2 uses the answer key or counters to check Player 1's answer. If it is correct, a marker is put on the same number on one of Player 1's bubbles.

If it is not correct, no marker is put down. If it already has been covered, no marker is put down.

Then the card is put on the red Card Pile, and it is Player 2's turn.

Players take turns. If all of the cards in the green Card Pile are used, the cards in the red Card Pile are mixed and placed facedown on the green Card Pile.

The winner is the first player to cover all of the numbers on his or her bubbles.

Answer Key: Bubble Mania

1. 0	13. 3	25. 3
2. 2	14. 3	26. 9
3. 4	15. 1	27. 5
4. 7	16. 0	28. 1
5. 6	17. 5	29. 5
6. 4	18. 8	30. 6
7. 1	19. 8	31. 6
8. 6	20. 4	32. 0
9. 5	21. 3	33. 2
10. 9	22. 8	34. 9
11. 2	23. 7	35. 2
12. 7	24. 4	36. 7

Variation

The player must give the answer to the subtraction problem and then give the subtraction equation that is related to the problem. For example, if the card shows "9 – 1," then the player says "9 – 1 = 8, and 9 – 8 = 1."

1.

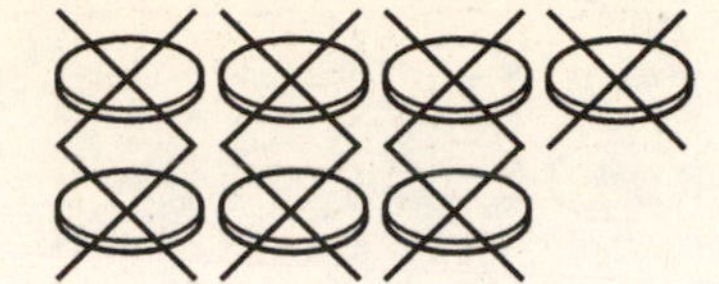

$7 - 7 =$ ____

2.

$6 - 4 =$ ____

Bubble Mania

3.

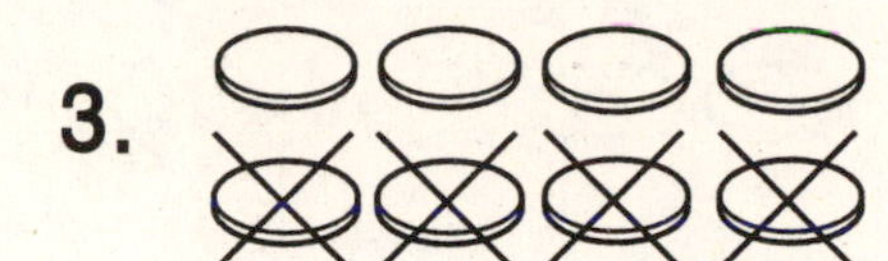

$8 - 4 =$ ____

Bubble Mania

4.

$10 - 3 =$ ____

Bubble Mania

5.

$7 - 1 =$ ____

Bubble Mania

6.

$9 - 5 =$ ____

Bubble Mania

7.

$3 - 2 =$ ____

Bubble Mania

8.

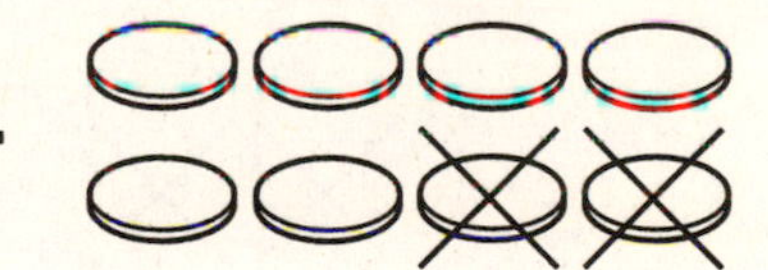

$8 - 2 =$ ____

Bubble Mania

9.

$10 - 5 =$ ____

Bubble Mania

10.

$9 - 0 =$ ____

Bubble Mania

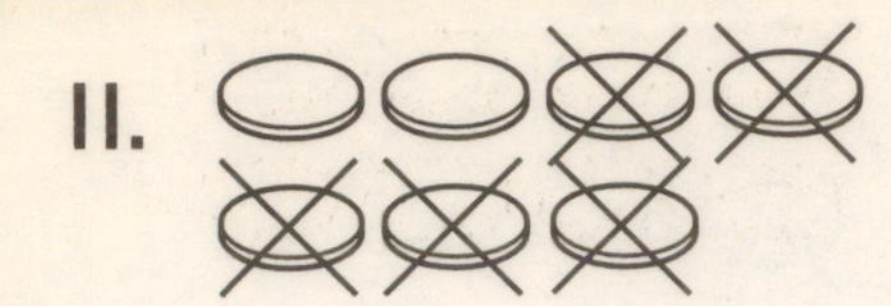

11.

$7 - 5 =$

Bubble Mania

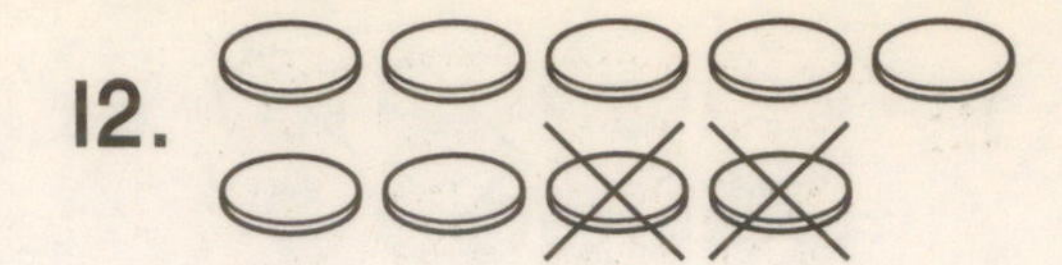

12.

$9 - 2 =$

Bubble Mania

13.

$9 - 6 =$

Bubble Mania

14.

$5 - 2 =$

Bubble Mania

15.

$8 - 7 =$

Bubble Mania

16.

$6 - 6 =$

Bubble Mania

17.

$9 - 4 =$

Bubble Mania

18.

$9 - 1 =$

Bubble Mania

19.

$10 - 2 =$

Bubble Mania

20.

$5 - 1 =$

Bubble Mania

21.

$8 - 5 =$

Bubble Mania

22.

$8 - 0 =$

Bubble Mania

23.

$8 - 1 =$

Bubble Mania

24. 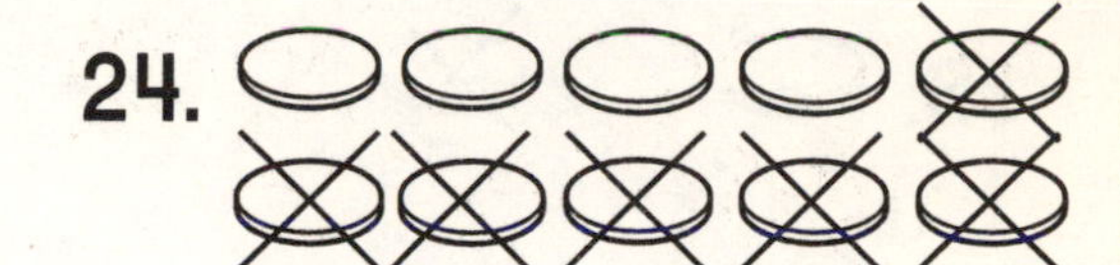

$10 - 6 =$

Bubble Mania

25.

$6 - 3 =$

Bubble Mania

26. 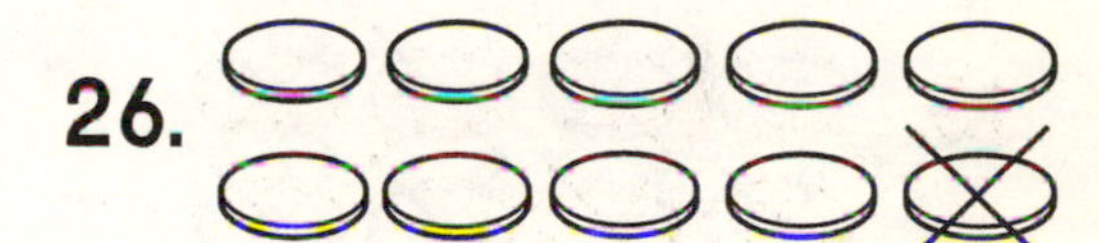

$10 - 1 =$

Bubble Mania

27.

$5 - 0 =$

Bubble Mania

28. 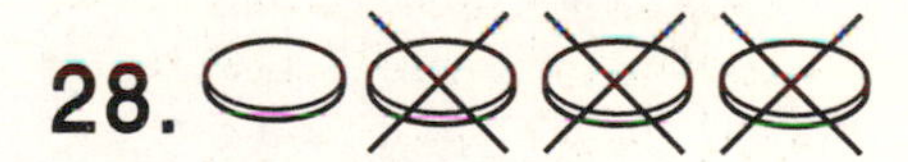

$4 - 3 =$

Bubble Mania

29.

$8 - 3 =$

Bubble Mania

30. 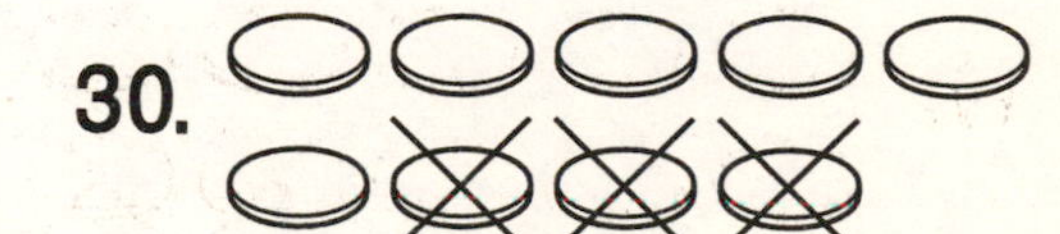

$9 - 3 =$

Bubble Mania

31. 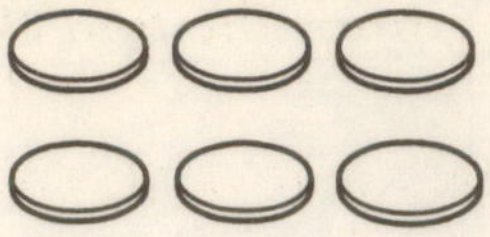 $6 - 0 =$ ____

Bubble Mania

32. 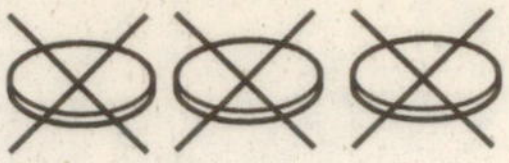 $3 - 3 =$ ____

Bubble Mania

33.  $3 - 1 =$ ____

Bubble Mania

34. 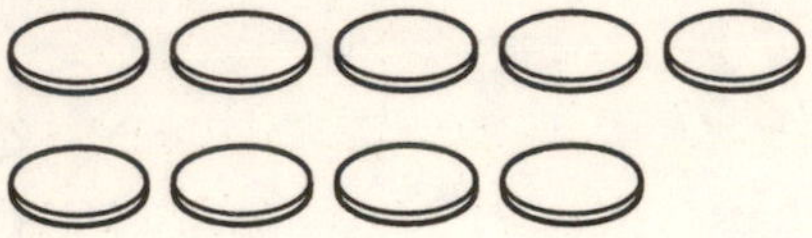 $9 - 0 =$ ____

Bubble Mania

35. 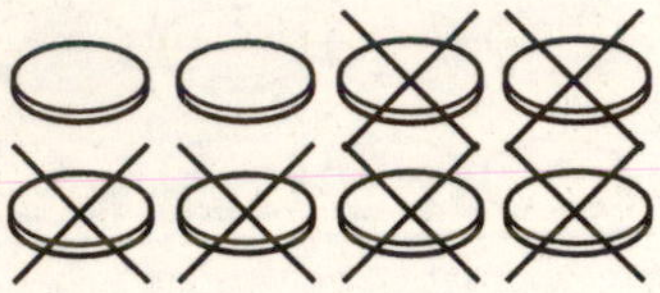 $8 - 6 =$ ____

Bubble Mania

36. 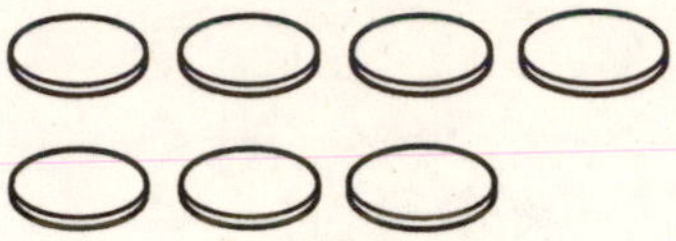 $7 - 0 =$ ____

Bubble Mania

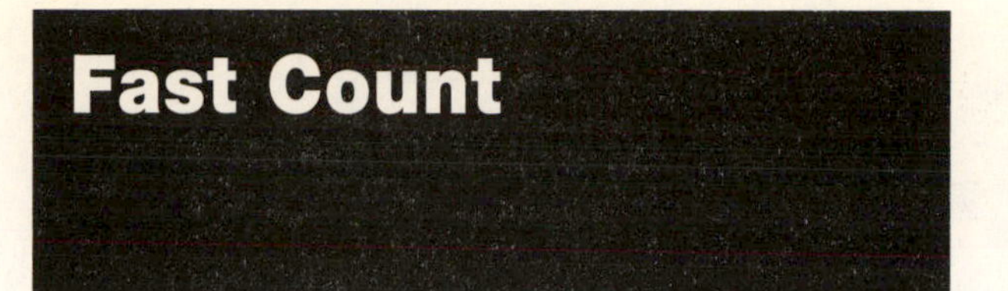

Objective: To reinforce the skill of skip counting to 100

Use with Kindergarten anytime after Chapter 12, Lesson 12-5; Grade 1, anytime after Chapter 7, Lesson 7-8; Grade 2, anytime after Chapter 3, Lesson 3-8.

You Will Need

Fast Count game cards (32)
- Cards 1–16 are answer cards
- Cards 17–32 are question cards
- **Teacher's Note:** You may want to use a different color for each set of game cards.

Fast Count answer key *or* Hundred Chart, page 66

1 number cube

How to Start

Two Players

Each player tosses the number cube. The player who tosses the greater number is Player 1 and starts the game.

Player 2 places the answer cards (1–16) in rows faceup between the players. Then Player 2 mixes the question cards (17–32) and places them facedown in a card pile.

How to Play

Fast Count is a matching game.

Player 1 takes the top question card from the pile, checks the number of dots on each domino—2, 5, or 10, and skip counts using that number. To make a match, the player checks for an answer card with the number that tells how many dots in all.

If a match is made, Player 2 uses the answer key or the Hundred Chart to check Player 1's match. If it is correct, Player 1 picks up both cards and places the pair aside.

If it is not correct, Player 1 puts the question card facedown at the bottom of the card pile.

Then it is Player 2's turn.

Players take turns.

The game ends when there are no cards left. The winner is the player with more pairs.

Answer Key: Fast Count

Card	matches	Card
1.		17.
2.		18.
3.		19.
4.		20.
5.		21.
6.		22.
7.		23.
8.		24.
9.		25.
10.		26.
11.		27.
12.		28.
13.		29.
14.		30.
15.		31.
16.		32.

1	2	3	4	5	6	7	8	9	10
11	12	13	14	15	16	17	18	19	20
21	22	23	24	25	26	27	28	29	30
31	32	33	34	35	36	37	38	39	40
41	42	43	44	45	46	47	48	49	50
51	52	53	54	55	56	57	58	59	60
61	62	63	64	65	66	67	68	69	70
71	72	73	74	75	76	77	78	79	80
81	82	83	84	85	86	87	88	89	90
91	92	93	94	95	96	97	98	99	100

1. 10 Fast Count	2. 15 Fast Count
3. 40 Fast Count	4. 8 Fast Count
5. 25 Fast Count	6. 30 Fast Count
7. 12 Fast Count	8. 20 Fast Count
9. 20 Fast Count	10. 14 Fast Count

11.

90

Fast Count

12.

55

Fast Count

13.

18

Fast Count

14.

22

Fast Count

15.

45

Fast Count

16.

60

Fast Count

17.

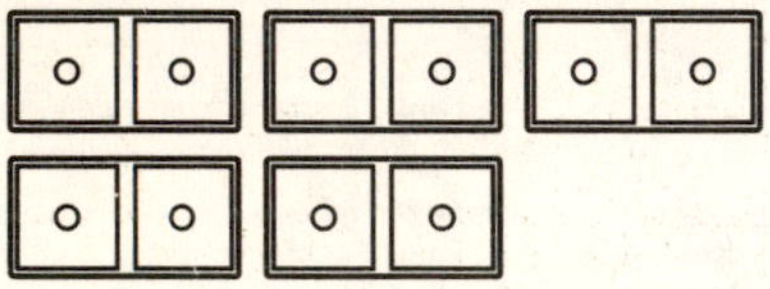

Fast Count

18.

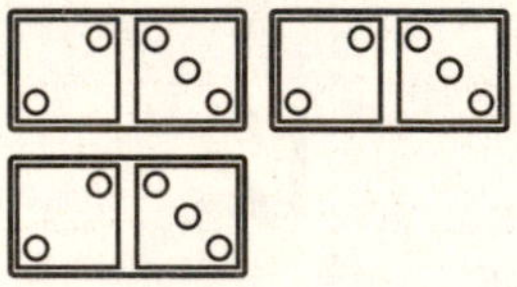

Fast Count

19.

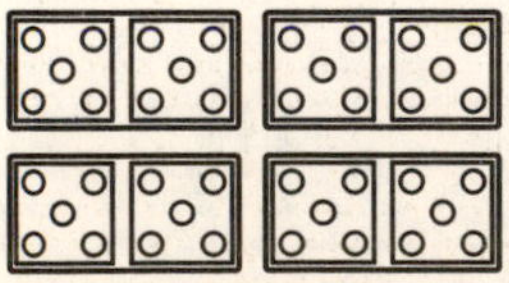

Fast Count

20.

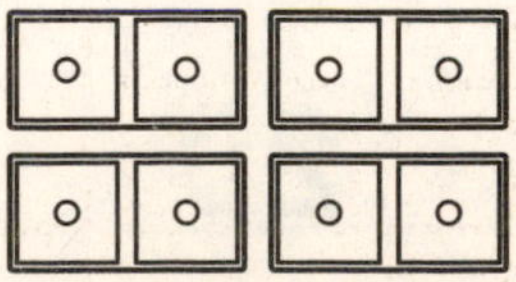

Fast Count

21.

Fast Count

22.

Fast Count

23.

Fast Count

24.

Fast Count

25.

Fast Count

26.

Fast Count

27.

Fast Count

28.

Fast Count

29.

Fast Count

30.

Fast Count

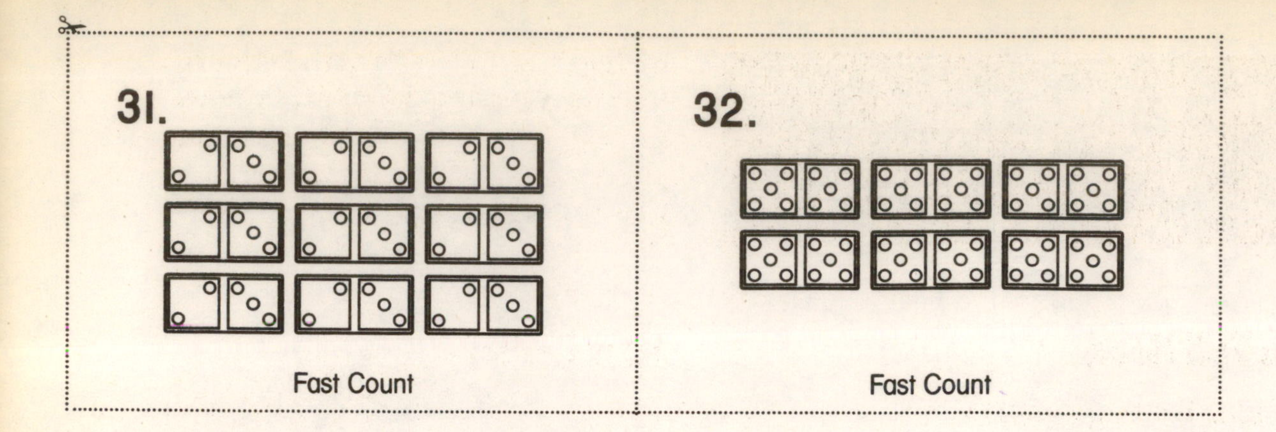
31.
Fast Count
32.
Fast Count

The Bear Facts

Objective: To reinforce the skills of finding sums and differences through 10

Use with Grade 1 anytime after Chapter 2, Lesson 2-9; Grade 2, anytime after Chapter 1, Lesson 1-10

You Will Need

Bear Facts game board

Bear Facts game cards (36)

Bear Facts answer key
or counters (10 for each player)

1 number cube

1 pawn for each player

How to Start

Two or Three Players

Each player tosses the number cube. The player who tosses the greatest number is Player 1.

Player 2 mixes the game cards and places them facedown on the green Card Pile on the game board.

Each player puts his or her pawn on Start at the beginning of the bear trail.

How to Play

Player 1 takes the top card from the green Card Pile, finds the sum or difference, and gives the answer.

Player 2 uses the answer key or counters to check Player 1's answer. If it is correct, Player 1 tosses the number cube and moves the same number of bear paw prints as the number shown on the cube.

If it is not correct, no move is made.

Then the card is placed on the red Card Pile, and it is Player 2's turn.

Players take turns. When a player lands on one of the lighter-colored paw prints, he or she must follow the directions given by the animal pointing to that paw print.

If all the cards are used, the cards in the red Card Pile are mixed and placed facedown on the green Card Pile.

The winner is the first player to land on Finish on the beehive. An exact toss of the cube is not needed.

Answer Key: The Bear Facts

1. 7
2. 8
3. 4
4. 8
5. 8
6. 9
7. 5
8. 3
9. 8
10. 0
11. 9
12. 5
13. 6
14. 8
15. 7
16. 9
17. 2
18. 7
19. 9
20. 2
21. 6
22. 6
23. 6
24. 5
25. 4
26. 6
27. 1
28. 5
29. 4
30. 5
31. 7
32. 3
33. 4
34. 4
35. 8
36. 7

Variation

If a player takes an addition card and gives the correct answer, he or she must say the other addition fact that is from the same family of facts ($3 + 7 = 10$ and $7 + 3 = 10$). If a player takes a subtraction card and gives the correct answer, he or she must tell the other subtraction fact from the same family of facts ($10 - 7 = 3$ and $10 - 3 = 7$). Players take turns.

1.

$3 + 4 =$

The Bear Facts

2.

$6 + 2 =$

The Bear Facts

3.

$7 - 3 =$

The Bear Facts

4.

$5 + 3 =$

The Bear Facts

5.

$10 - 2 =$

The Bear Facts

6.

$10 - 1 =$

The Bear Facts

7.

$7 - 2 =$

The Bear Facts

8.

$6 - 3 =$

The Bear Facts

9.

$4 + 4 =$

The Bear Facts

10.

$9 - 9 =$

The Bear Facts

11.

$9 + 0 =$ ▭

The Bear Facts

12.

$2 + 3 =$ ▭

The Bear Facts

13.

$3 + 3 =$ ▭

The Bear Facts

14.

$8 - 0 =$ ▭

The Bear Facts

15.

$4 + 3 =$ ▭

The Bear Facts

16.

$8 + 1 =$ ▭

The Bear Facts

17.

$5 - 3 =$ ▭

The Bear Facts

18.

$6 + 1 =$ ▭

The Bear Facts

19.

$4 + 5 =$ ▭

The Bear Facts

20.

$7 - 5 =$ ▭

The Bear Facts

21.

$9 - 3 =$ ☐

The Bear Facts

22.

$4 + 2 =$ ☐

The Bear Facts

23.

$8 - 2 =$ ☐

The Bear Facts

24.

$5 - 0 =$ ☐

The Bear Facts

25.

$9 - 5 =$ ☐

The Bear Facts

26.

$2 + 4 =$ ☐

The Bear Facts

27.

$8 - 7 =$ ☐

The Bear Facts

28.

$4 + 1 =$ ☐

The Bear Facts

29.

$6 - 2 =$ ☐

The Bear Facts

30.

$10 - 5 =$ ☐

The Bear Facts

31.

$2 + 5 =$ ____

The Bear Facts

32.

$8 - 5 =$ ____

The Bear Facts

33.

$2 + 2 =$ ____

The Bear Facts

34.

$10 - 6 =$ ____

The Bear Facts

35.

$0 + 8 =$ ____

The Bear Facts

36.

$10 - 3 =$ ____

The Bear Facts

Fraction Fun

Objective: To reinforce the skill of recognizing fractions

Use with Grade 1 anytime after Chapter 5, Lesson 5-12; Grade 2, anytime after Chapter 7, Lesson 7-10

You Will Need

Fraction Fun game cards (36)
Cards 1–18 are shape cards
Cards 19–38 are fraction cards
Teacher's Note: You may want to use a different color for each set of game cards.

Fraction Fun answer key
or fraction manipulatives for 1, $\frac{1}{2}$, $\frac{1}{3}$, and $\frac{1}{4}$ (1 set for each player)

1 number cube

How to Start

Two Players

Each player tosses the number cube. The player who tosses the lesser number is Player 1 and starts the game.

Player 2 mixes the fraction cards (19–38) and places them facedown in a pile between the two players. Then Player 2 mixes the shape cards (1–18) and gives 4 cards to each player. These cards are placed faceup in front of the players.

Each player takes 3 cards from the card pile and places them faceup in front of himself or herself.

How to Play

Fraction Fun is a matching game.

Player 1 takes the top card from the answer card pile, tells what part of a whole is shown, and checks for a match with any of the shape cards in front of himself or herself. A match is made when the shaded part of a shape on one card matches the fraction on the answer card.

If a match is made, Player 2 uses the answer key or fraction manipulatives to check Player 1's match. If it is correct, Player 1 takes both cards and puts the pair aside. Then Player 1 takes another card from the shape card pile to replace the missing card in front of himself or herself.

If no match is made, the card is placed faceup to begin a discard pile. Then it is Player 2's turn.

Players take turns. Players may take the top card from the answer card pile or the discard pile to make a match.

If a player picks a Crazy Card, he or she may use it right away or save it for another turn. Crazy Cards make a match with any card.

If all of the cards in the card pile are used, the cards in the discard pile are mixed and placed facedown to be used again.

The winner is the first player with 5 pairs of matching cards.

Answer Key: Fraction Fun

Card	matches	Cards
1.	$\frac{1}{2}$	20, 23, 27, 32, 35, 37
2.	$\frac{1}{4}$	19, 22, 26, 30, 31, 34
3.	$\frac{1}{3}$	21, 25, 29, 33, 36, 38
4.	$\frac{1}{2}$	20, 23, 27, 32, 35, 37
5.	$\frac{1}{3}$	21, 25, 29, 33, 36, 38
6.	$\frac{1}{2}$	20, 23, 27, 32, 35, 37
7.	$\frac{1}{4}$	19, 22, 26, 30, 31, 34
8.	$\frac{1}{3}$	21, 25, 29, 33, 36, 38
9.	$\frac{1}{2}$	20, 23, 27, 32, 35, 37
10.	$\frac{1}{2}$	20, 23, 27, 32, 35, 37
11.	$\frac{1}{4}$	19, 22, 26, 30, 31, 34
12.	$\frac{1}{4}$	19, 22, 26, 30, 31, 34
13.	$\frac{1}{2}$	20, 23, 27, 32,35, 37
14.	$\frac{1}{3}$	21, 25, 29,33, 36, 38
15.	$\frac{1}{4}$	19, 22, 26, 30, 31, 34
16.	$\frac{1}{3}$	21, 25, 29, 33, 36, 38
17.	$\frac{1}{4}$	19, 22, 26, 30, 31, 34
18.	$\frac{1}{3}$	21, 25, 29, 33, 36, 38

Variation

A player may match the cards in front of the other player but must replace his or her card with one from the card pile.

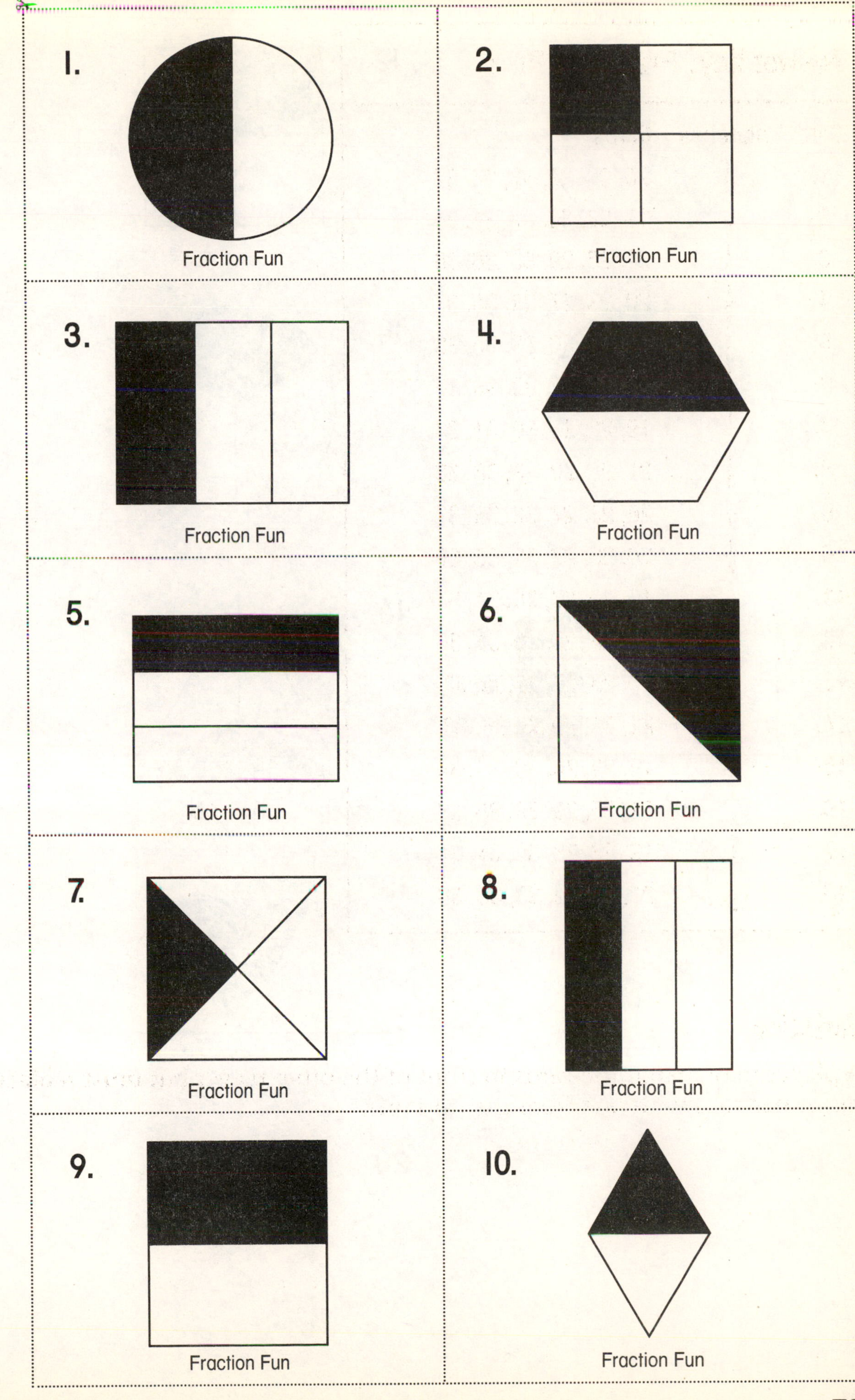
1.
Fraction Fun
2.
Fraction Fun
3.
Fraction Fun
4.
Fraction Fun
5.
Fraction Fun
6.
Fraction Fun
7.
Fraction Fun
8.
Fraction Fun
9.
Fraction Fun
10.
Fraction Fun

11.

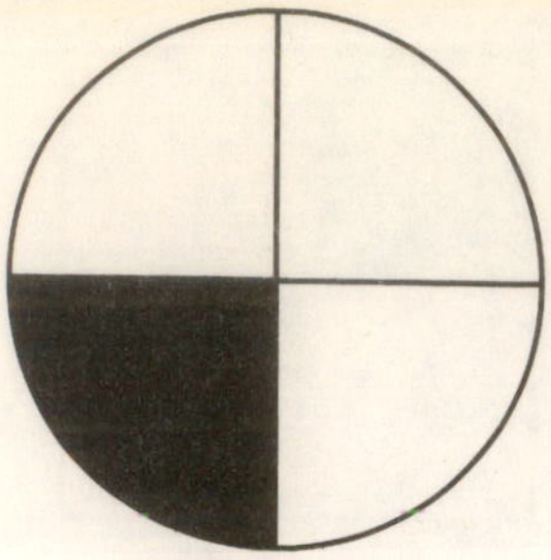

Fraction Fun

12.

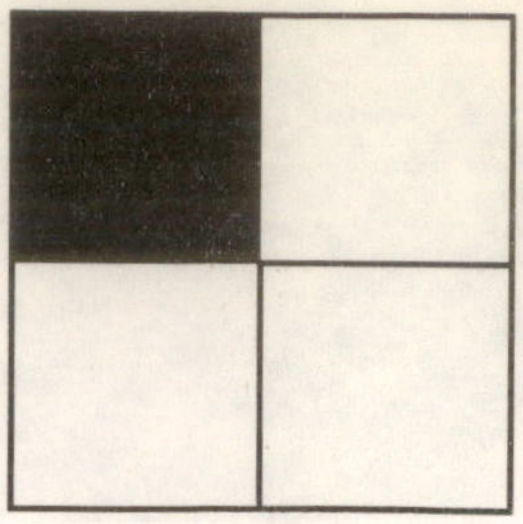

Fraction Fun

13.

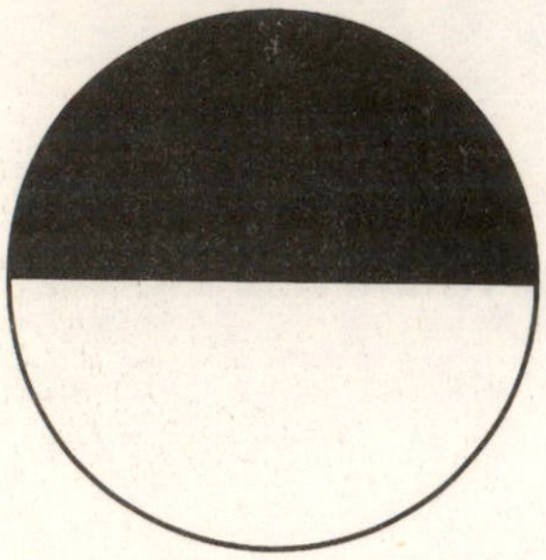

Fraction Fun

14.

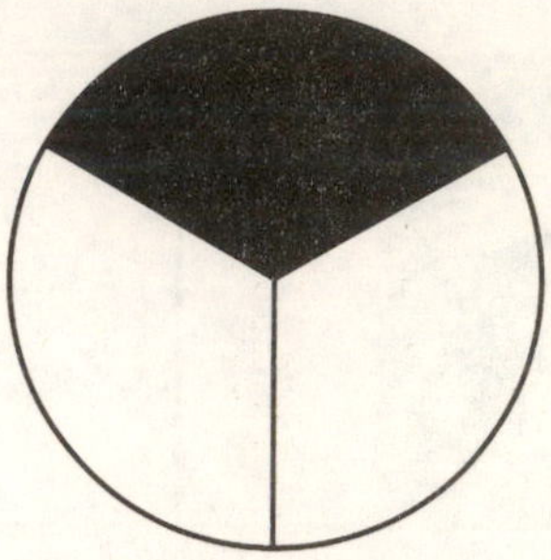

Fraction Fun

15.

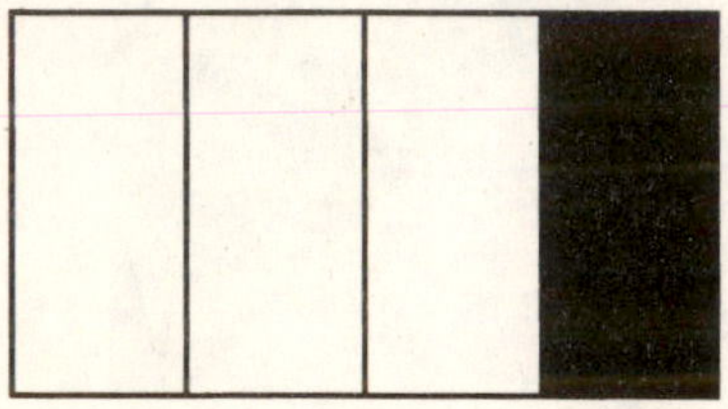

Fraction Fun

16.

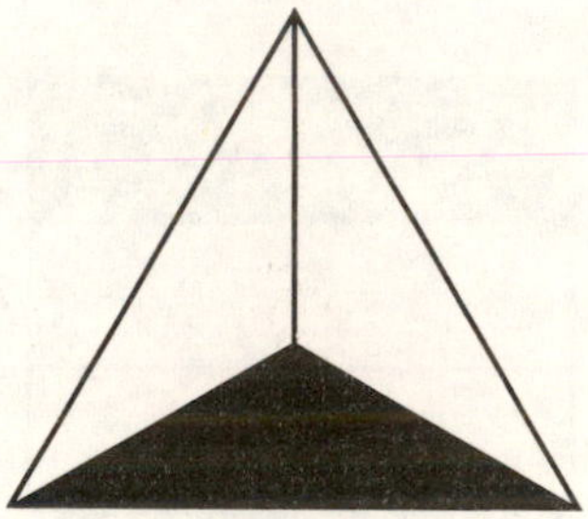

Fraction Fun

17.

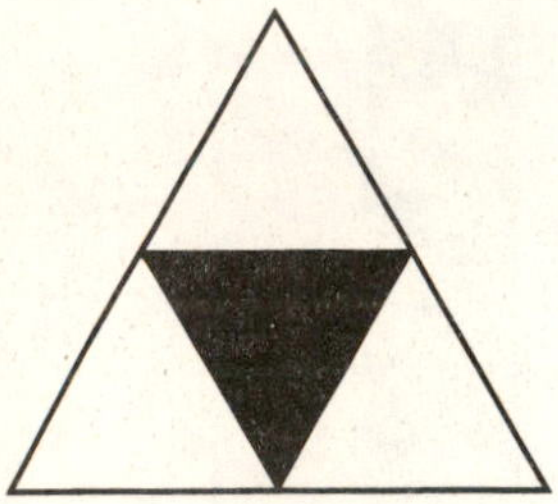

Fraction Fun

18.

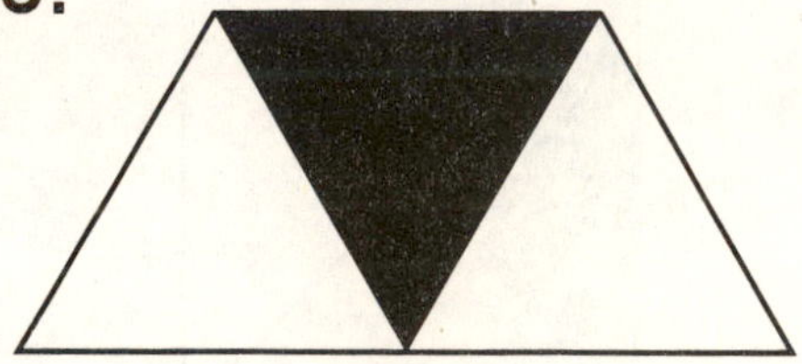

Fraction Fun

19.

$\frac{1}{4}$

Fraction Fun

20.

$\frac{1}{2}$

Fraction Fun

21. $\frac{1}{3}$ Fraction Fun	22. $\frac{1}{4}$ Fraction Fun
23. $\frac{1}{2}$ Fraction Fun	24. crazy card Fraction Fun
25. $\frac{1}{3}$ Fraction Fun	26. $\frac{1}{4}$ Fraction Fun
27. $\frac{1}{2}$ Fraction Fun	28. crazy card Fraction Fun
29. $\frac{1}{3}$ Fraction Fun	30. $\frac{1}{4}$ Fraction Fun

31. $\frac{1}{4}$ Fraction Fun	32. $\frac{1}{2}$ Fraction Fun
33. $\frac{1}{3}$ Fraction Fun	34. $\frac{1}{4}$ Fraction Fun
35. $\frac{1}{2}$ Fraction Fun	36. $\frac{1}{3}$ Fraction Fun
37. $\frac{1}{2}$ Fraction Fun	38. $\frac{1}{3}$ Fraction Fun

Time's Up

Objective: To reinforce the skill of telling time to the hour and half hour

Use with Grade 1 anytime after Chapter 6, Lesson 6-4; Grade 2, anytime after Chapter 8, Lesson 8-1

You Will Need

- Time's Up game board
- Time's Up game cards (36)
- Time's Up answer key
- 1 number cube
- 20 round markers in 2 colors (10 of each color)

How to Start

Two Players

Each player tosses the number cube. The player who tosses the lesser number is Player 1 and starts the game.

Player 2 mixes the game cards and places them facedown on the green Card Pile on the game board.

Each player starts with 10 round markers of 1color.

How to Play

Player 1 takes the top card from the green Card Pile, reads the time, and finds a clock that shows that time on one of his or her balloons.

Player 2 uses the answer key to check Player 1's answer. If it is correct, a marker is put on the clock that shows that time. If it is not correct, no marker is put down. If it already has been covered or is not there, no marker is put down.

Then the card is placed facedown on the red Card Pile, and it is Player 2's turn.

Players take turns. If a player picks a Crazy Card, the player can use it to put a marker on any of his or her clocks. The Crazy Card can be used right away or saved to be used on another turn.

If all of the cards in the green card pile are used, the cards in the red Card Pile are mixed and placed facedown on the green card pile.

The winner is the first player to cover all of the clocks on his or her balloons.

Answer Key: Time's Up

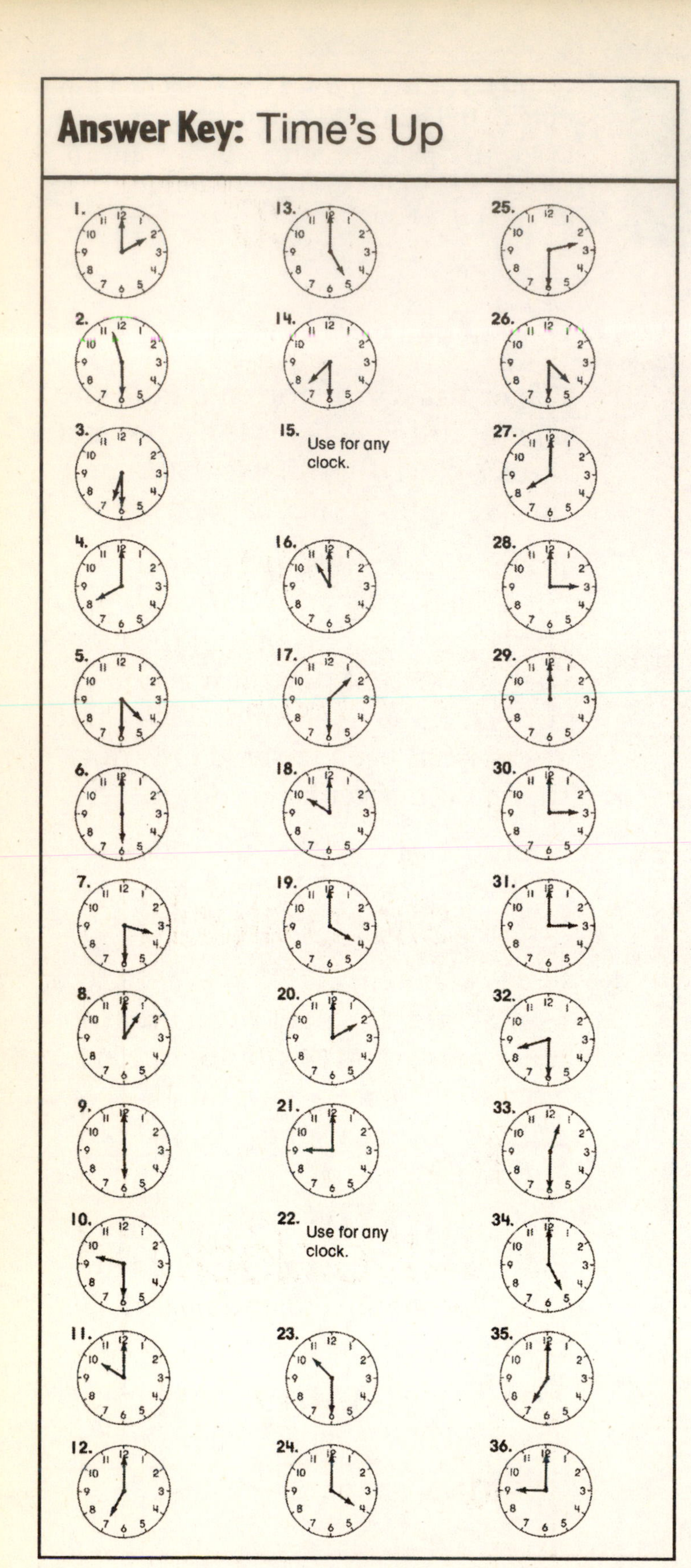

1. 2:00 Time's Up	2. 11:30 Time's Up
3. 6:30 Time's Up	4. 8:00 Time's Up
5. 4:30 Time's Up	6. six o'clock Time's Up
7. 3:30 Time's Up	8. 1 o'clock Time's Up
9. 6:00 Time's Up	10. 9:30 Time's Up

11. ten o'clock Time's Up	12. 7:00 Time's Up
13. 5:00 Time's Up	14. 7:30 Time's Up
15. crazy card Time's Up	16. 11 o'clock Time's Up
17. 1:30 Time's Up	18. 10:00 Time's Up
19. 4 o'clock Time's Up	20. two o'clock Time's Up

21. 9:00 Time's Up	22. crazy card Time's Up
23. 10:30 Time's Up	24. 4:00 Time's Up
25. 2:30 Time's Up	26. 4:30 Time's Up
27. 8 o'clock Time's Up	28. 3 o'clock Time's Up
29. 12:00 Time's Up	30. three o'clock Time's Up

31. 3 o'clock Time's Up	32. 8:30 Time's Up
33. 12:30 Time's Up	34. 5:00 Time's Up
35. 7 o'clock Time's Up	36. nine o'clock Time's Up

High-Rise Math

Objective: To reinforce the skill of using ordinal numbers through tenth to identify position

Use with Grade 1 anytime after Chapter 7, Lesson 7-12; Grade 2, anytime after Chapter 3, Lesson 3-10

You Will Need

High-Rise Math game board
High-Rise Math game cards (36)
High-Rise Math answer key
1 number cube
20 round markers in 2 colors
(10 of each color)

How to Start

Two Players

Each player tosses the number cube. The player who tosses the greater number is Player 1 and starts the game.

Player 2 mixes the game cards and places them facedown on the green Card Pile on the game board.

Each player starts with 10 round markers of 1 color.

How to Play

Player 1 takes the top card from the green Card Pile, finds which X is circled by counting from the left, and says the ordinal number.

Player 2 uses the answer key to check Player 1's answer. If it is correct, a marker is placed on the same ordinal number marking one of the floors in his or her high-rise building.

If it is not correct, no marker is put down. If it already has been covered, no marker is put down.

Then the card is put on the red Card Pile, and it is Player 2's turn.

Players take turns. If all of the cards in the green Card Pile are used, the cards in the red Card Pile are mixed and placed facedown on the green Card Pile.

The game ends when one of the players covers all of the floors in his or her high-rise building, or if there are no cards left. The winner is the player with more of his or her floors covered.

Answer Key: High-Rise Math

1. first
2. sixth
3. second
4. eighth
5. fifth
6. eighth
7. ninth
8. fourth
9. first
10. seventh
11. third
12. fourth
13. sixth
14. third
15. ninth
16. second
17. seventh
18. fifth
19. eighth
20. fifth
21. tenth
22. first
23. third
24. fourth
25. sixth
26. second
27. ninth
28. tenth
29. fourth
30. fifth
31. seventh
32. eighth
33. tenth
34. third
35. seventh
36. sixth

1.

(X) X X X X X X X X X

High-Rise Math

2.

X X X X X (X) X X X X

High-Rise Math

3.

X (X) X X X X X X X X

High-Rise Math

4.

X X X X X X X (X) X X

High-Rise Math

5.

X X X X (X) X X X X X

High-Rise Math

6.

X X X X X X X (X) X X

High-Rise Math

7.

X X X X X X X X (X) X

High-Rise Math

8.

X X X (X) X X X X X X

High-Rise Math

9.

(X) X X X X X X X X X

High-Rise Math

10.

X X X X X X (X) X X X

High-Rise Math

11.

X X (X) X X X X X X X

High-Rise Math

12.

X X X (X) X X X X X X

High-Rise Math

13.

X X X X X (X) X X X X

High-Rise Math

14.

X X (X) X X X X X X X

High-Rise Math

15.

X X X X X X X X (X) X

High-Rise Math

16.

X (X) X X X X X X X X

High-Rise Math

17.

X X X X X X (X) X X X

High-Rise Math

18.

X X X X (X) X X X X X

High-Rise Math

19.

X X X X X X X (X) X X

High-Rise Math

20.

X X X X (X) X X X X X

High-Rise Math

21.

X X X X X X X X X (X)

High-Rise Math

22.

(X) X X X X X X X X X

High-Rise Math

23.

X X (X) X X X X X X X

High-Rise Math

24.

X X X (X) X X X X X X

High-Rise Math

25.

X X X X X (X) X X X X

High-Rise Math

26.

X (X) X X X X X X X X

High-Rise Math

27.

X X X X X X X X (X) X

High-Rise Math

28.

X X X X X X X X X (X)

High-Rise Math

29.

X X X (X) X X X X X X

High-Rise Math

30.

X X X X (X) X X X X X

High-Rise Math

31.

X X X X X X (X) X X X

High-Rise Math

32.

X X X X X X X (X) X X

High-Rise Math

33.

X X X X X X X X X (X)

High-Rise Math

34.

X X (X) X X X X X X X

High-Rise Math

35.

X X X X X X (X) X X X

High-Rise Math

36.

X X X X X (X) X X X X

High-Rise Math

Picking Favorites

Objective: To reinforce the understanding of bar graphs

Use with Grade 1 anytime after Chapter 8, Lesson 8-13; Grade 2, anytime after Chapter 8, Lesson 8-13

You Will Need

Picking Favorites game cards (36)
- Cards 1–18 are graph cards
- Cards 19–36 are picture cards
- **Teacher's Note:** You may want to use a different color for each set of game cards.

Picking Favorites answer key

1 number cube

How to Start

Two Players

Each player tosses the number cube. The player who tosses the lesser number is Player 1 and starts the game.

Player 2 places the picture cards (19–36) faceup in rows between the players. Then Player 2 mixes the graph cards (1–18) and places them facedown in a card pile between the players.

How to Play

Picking Favorites is a matching game.

Player 1 takes the top graph card from the card pile, looks at the bar graph, identifies the favorite item, and checks the picture cards for a match. A match is made when the item selected the greatest number of times on the bar graph matches the picture of the favorite item on a picture card.

If a match is made, Player 2 uses the answer key to check Player 1's match. If it is correct, Player 1 takes both cards and places them aside.

If it is not correct, the graph card is placed facedown at the bottom of the card pile.

Then it is Player 2's turn.

Players take turns.

The game ends when there are no cards left in the card pile. The winner is the player with more pairs.

Answer Key: Picking Favorites

Card	matches	Card
1.		19.
2.		20.
3.		21.
4.		22.
5.		23.
6.		24.
7.		25.
8.		26.
9.		27.
10.		28.
11.		29.
12.		30.
13.		31.
14.		32.
15.		33.
16.		34.
17.		35.
18.		36.

1. Sport

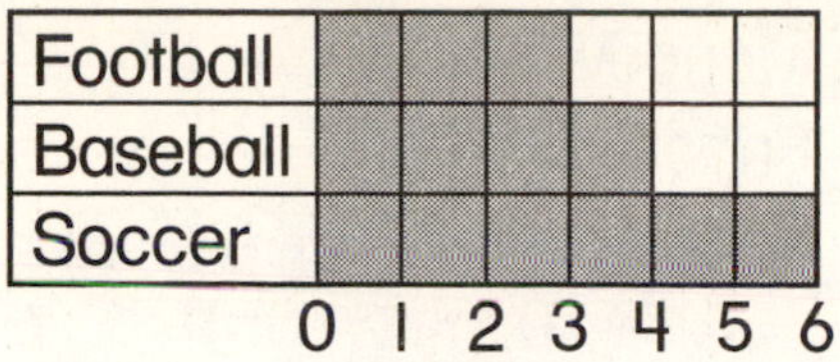

Football
Baseball
Soccer

0 1 2 3 4 5 6

Picking Favorites

2. Place

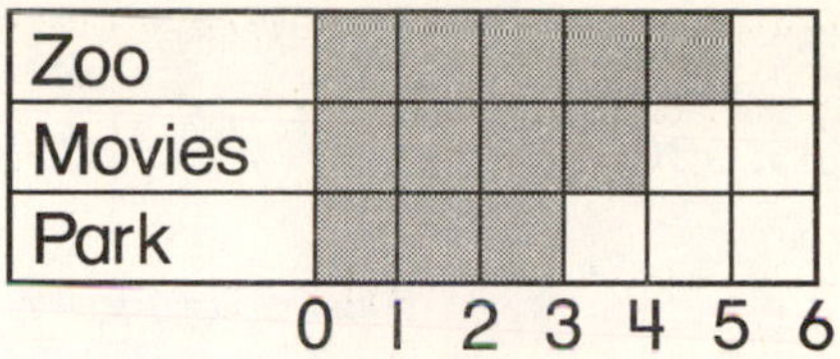

Zoo
Movies
Park

0 1 2 3 4 5 6

Picking Favorites

3. Toy

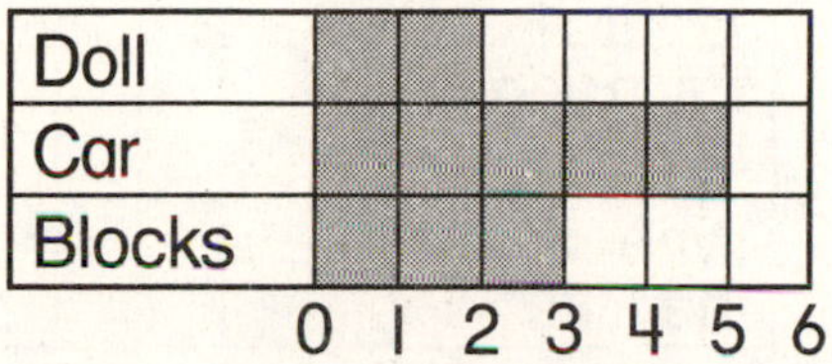

Doll
Car
Blocks

0 1 2 3 4 5 6

Picking Favorites

4. Pet

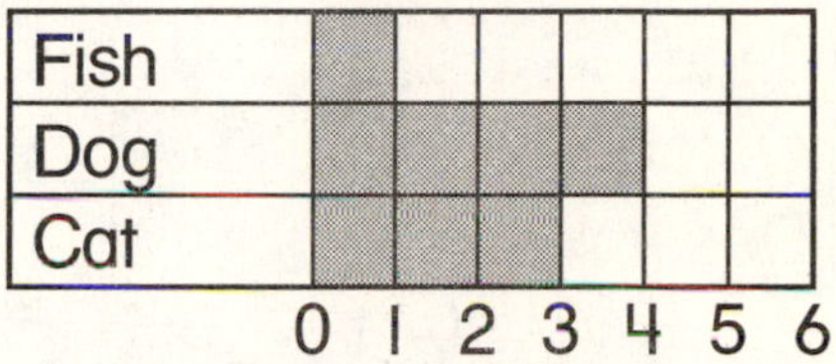

Fish
Dog
Cat

0 1 2 3 4 5 6

Picking Favorites

5. Zoo Animal

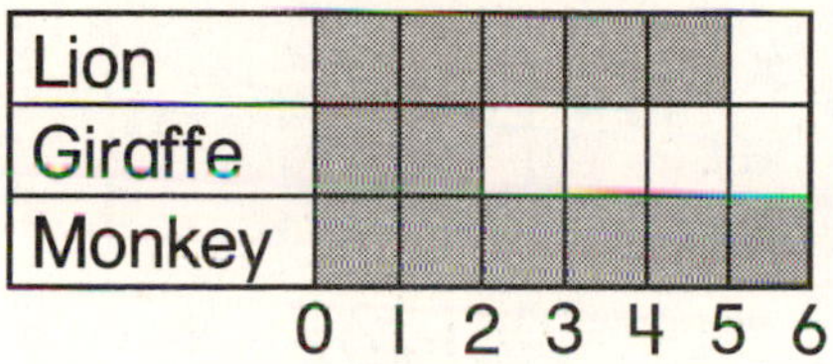

Lion
Giraffe
Monkey

0 1 2 3 4 5 6

Picking Favorites

6. Fruit

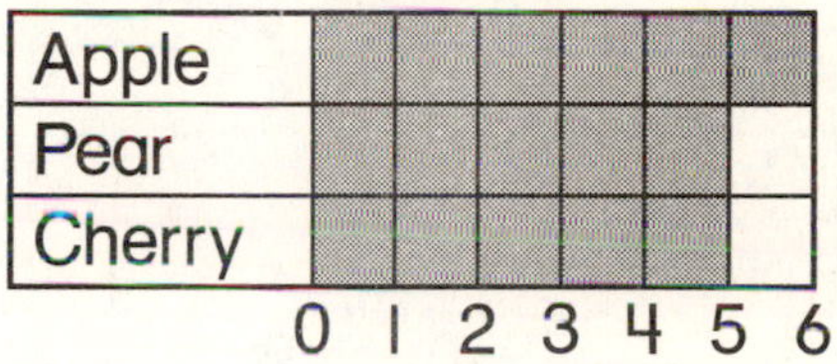

Apple
Pear
Cherry

0 1 2 3 4 5 6

Same Shape

7. Lunch

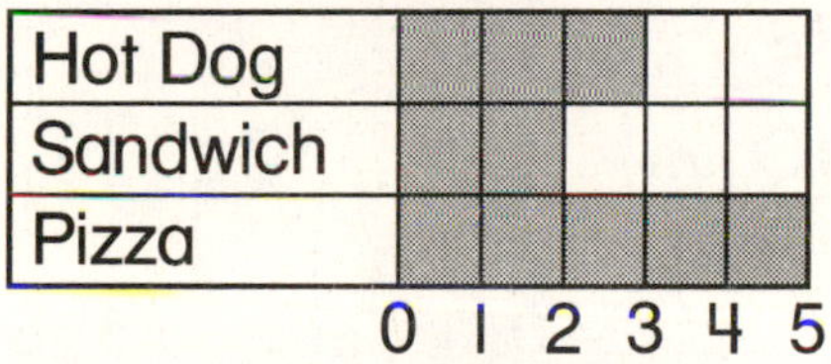

Hot Dog
Sandwich
Pizza

0 1 2 3 4 5

Picking Favorites

8. Dessert

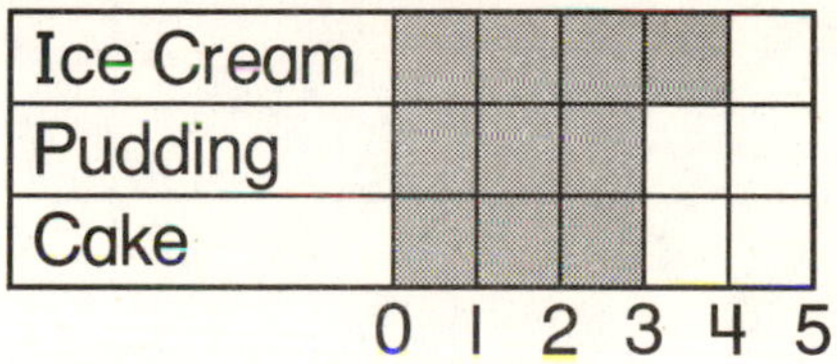

Ice Cream
Pudding
Cake

0 1 2 3 4 5

Picking Favorites

9. Insect

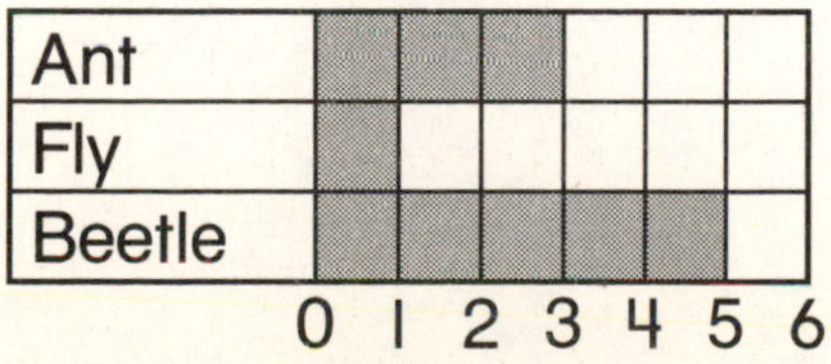

Ant
Fly
Beetle

0 1 2 3 4 5 6

Picking Favorites

10. Shape

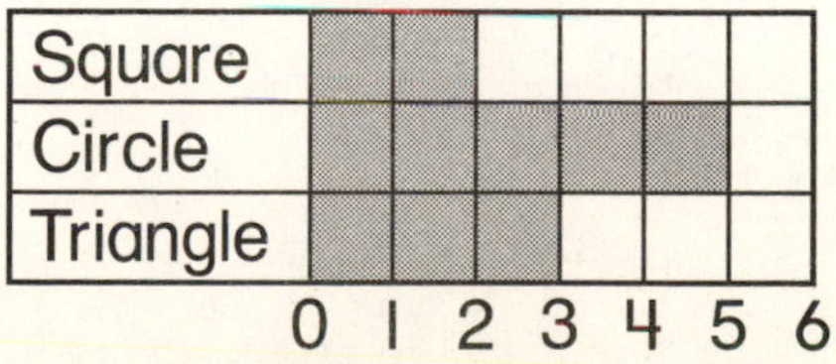

Square
Circle
Triangle

0 1 2 3 4 5 6

Picking Favorites

11.

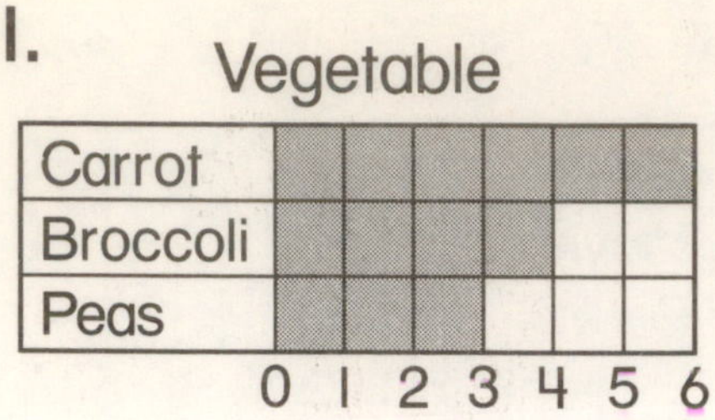

Vegetable

Carrot
Broccoli
Peas

0 1 2 3 4 5 6

Picking Favorites

12.

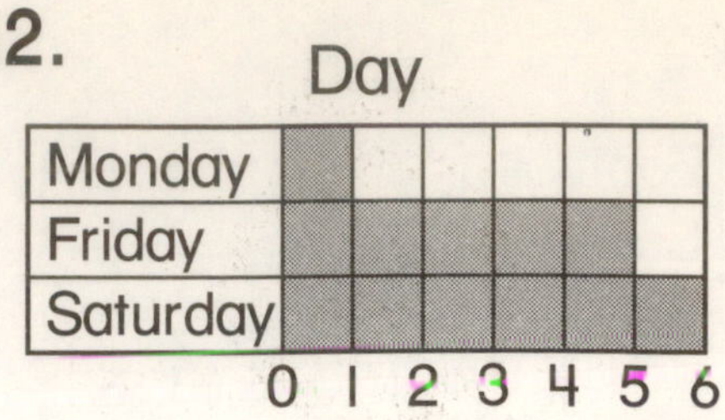

Day

Monday
Friday
Saturday

0 1 2 3 4 5 6

Picking Favorites

13.

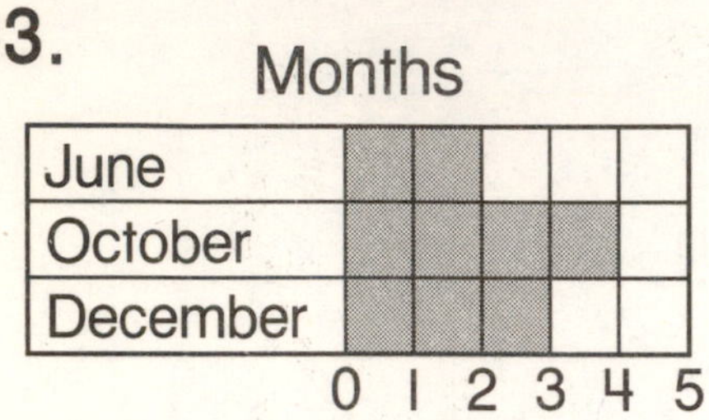

Months

June
October
December

0 1 2 3 4 5

Picking Favorites

14.

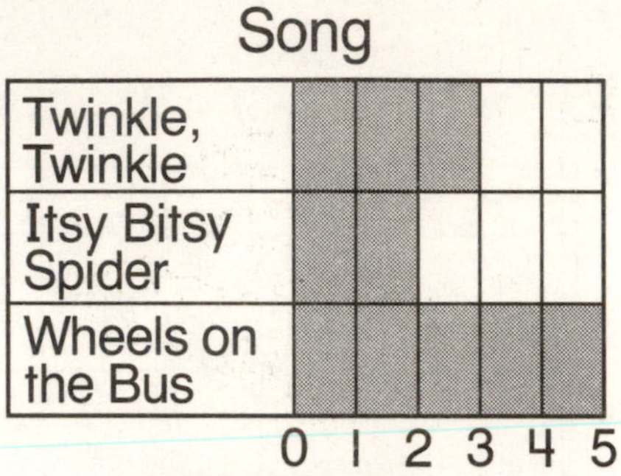

Song

Twinkle, Twinkle
Itsy Bitsy Spider
Wheels on the Bus

0 1 2 3 4 5

Picking Favorites

15.

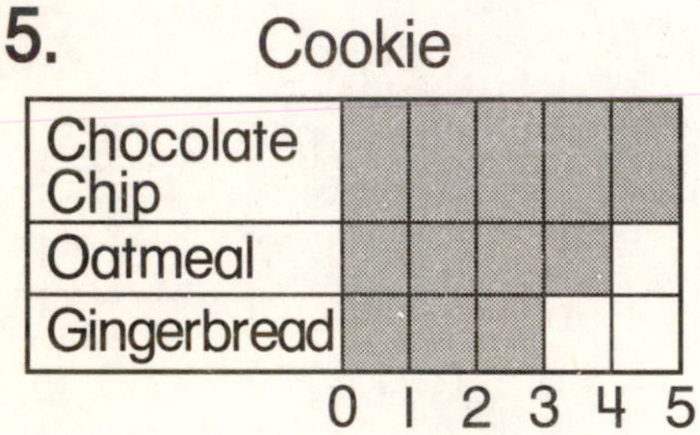

Cookie

Chocolate Chip
Oatmeal
Gingerbread

0 1 2 3 4 5

Picking Favorites

16.

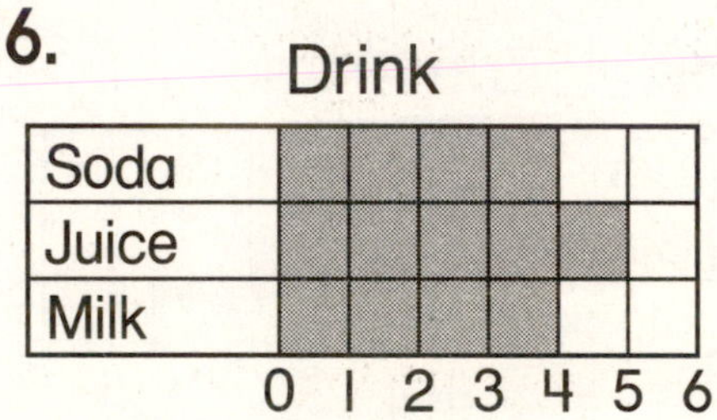

Drink

Soda
Juice
Milk

0 1 2 3 4 5 6

Picking Favorites

17.

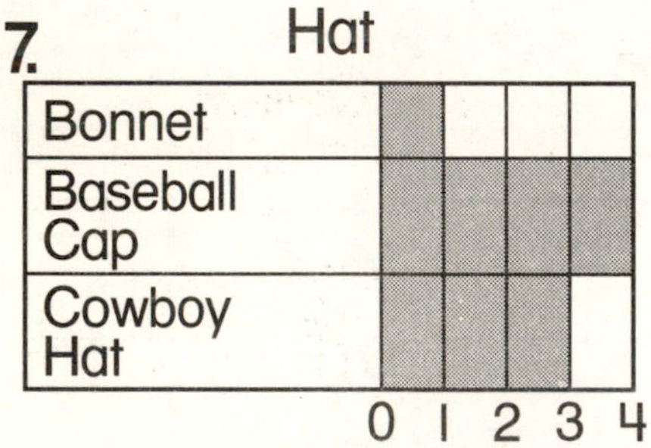

Hat

Bonnet
Baseball Cap
Cowboy Hat

0 1 2 3 4

Picking Favorites

18.

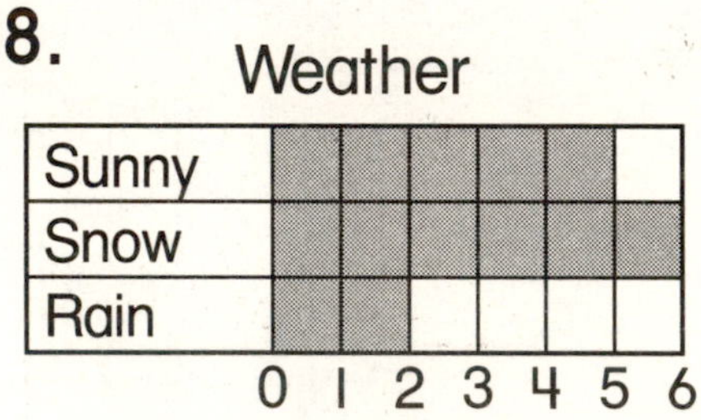

Weather

Sunny
Snow
Rain

0 1 2 3 4 5 6

Picking Favorites

19.
Soccer
Picking Favorites

20.
Zoo
Picking Favorites

21.
Car
Picking Favorites

22.
Dog
Picking Favorites

23.
Monkey
Picking Favorites

24.
Apple
Same Shape

25.
Pizza
Picking Favorites

26.
Ice Cream
Picking Favorites

27.
Beetle
Picking Favorites

28.
Circle
Picking Favorites

29.

Carrot

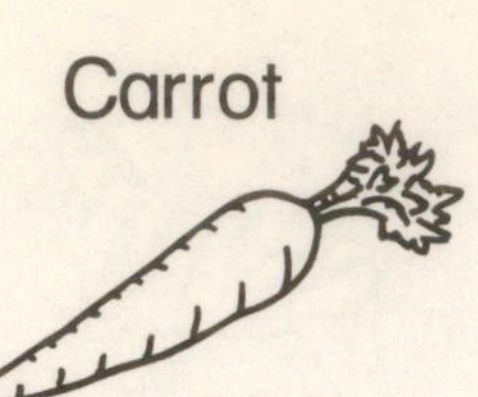

Picking Favorites

30.

Saturday

iday	Saturday
3	4
	11

Picking Favorites

31.

October

Picking Favorites

32.

Wheels on the Bus

Picking Favorites

33.

Chocolate Chip

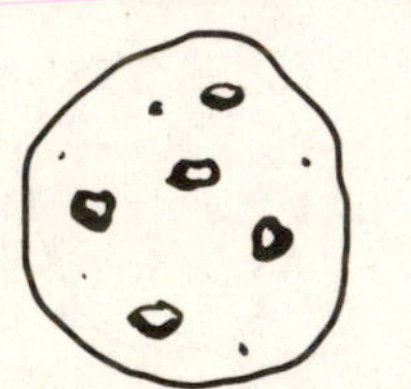

Picking Favorites

34.

Juice

Picking Favorites

35.

Baseball Cap

Picking Favorites

36.

Snow

Picking Favorites

Shopping Spree

Objective: To reinforce the skill of matching coin values with prices

Use with Grade 1 anytime after Chapter 9, Lesson 9-7; Grade 2, anytime after Chapter 3, Lesson 3-14

You Will Need

Shopping Spree game cards (40)
Cards 1–20 are price tag cards
Cards 21–40 are coin cards
Teacher's Note: You may want to use a different color for each set of game cards.

Shopping Spree answer key *or* coins (1 quarter, 5 dimes, 6 nickels, and 10 pennies for each player)

1 number cube

How to Start

Two Players

Each player tosses the number cube. The player with the greater number is Player 1 and starts the game.

Player 2 places the price tag cards (1–20) faceup in 4 rows with 5 cards in each row. Then Player 2 mixes the coin cards (21–40) and places them facedown in a card pile.

How to Play

Player 1 takes the top coin card from the card pile, finds the total value of the coins on the card, and chooses the card with the price tag that matches the total value of coins.

Player 2 uses the answer key or coins to check Player 1's match. If it is correct, Player 1 places the price tag card facedown in its place and keeps the coin card.

If it is not correct, Player 1 returns the price tag card faceup to its place and the coin card to the bottom of the card pile.

Players take turns.

The game ends when all of the price tag cards are facedown. The winner is the player with the most coin cards.

Answer Key: Shopping Spree

Card	matches	Card
1.		22.
2.		23.
3.		25.
4.		24.
5.		30.
6.		40.
7.		34.
8.		26.
9.		28.
10.		31.
11.		27.
12.		32.
13.		33.
14.		29.
15.		35.
16.		36.
17.		21.
18.		37.
19.		38.
20.		39.

Variation

All of the game cards are mixed and placed facedown in 5 rows with 8 cards in each row. Players take turns turning over 2 cards to try to make a match. If a match is made, the player may keep the pair of cards. If a match is not made, the player returns the cards to their original places. The player with more pairs wins.

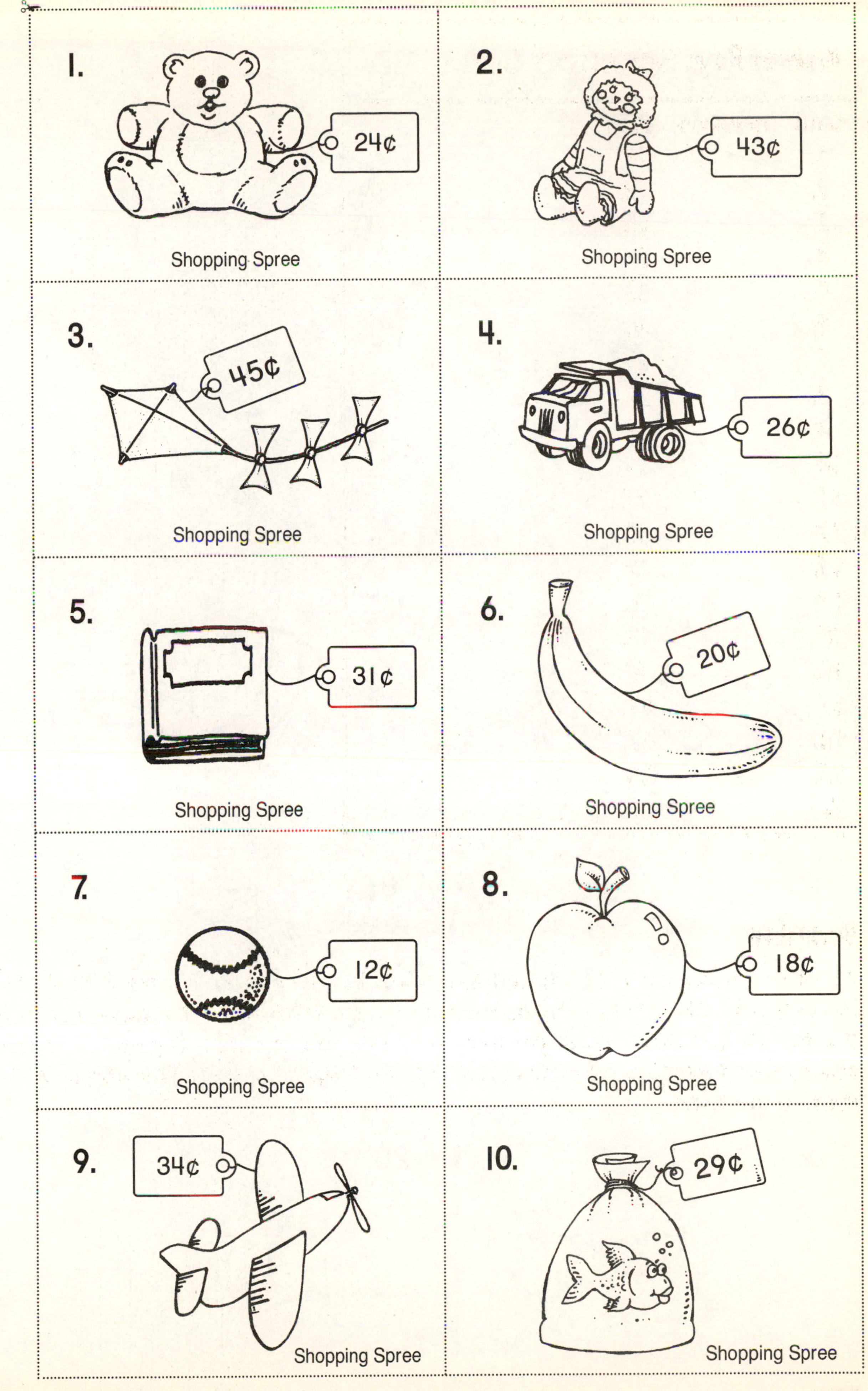
1.
24¢
Shopping Spree
2.
43¢
Shopping Spree
3.
45¢
Shopping Spree
4.
26¢
Shopping Spree
5.
31¢
Shopping Spree
6.
20¢
Shopping Spree
7.
12¢
Shopping Spree
8.
18¢
Shopping Spree
9.
34¢
Shopping Spree
10.
29¢
Shopping Spree

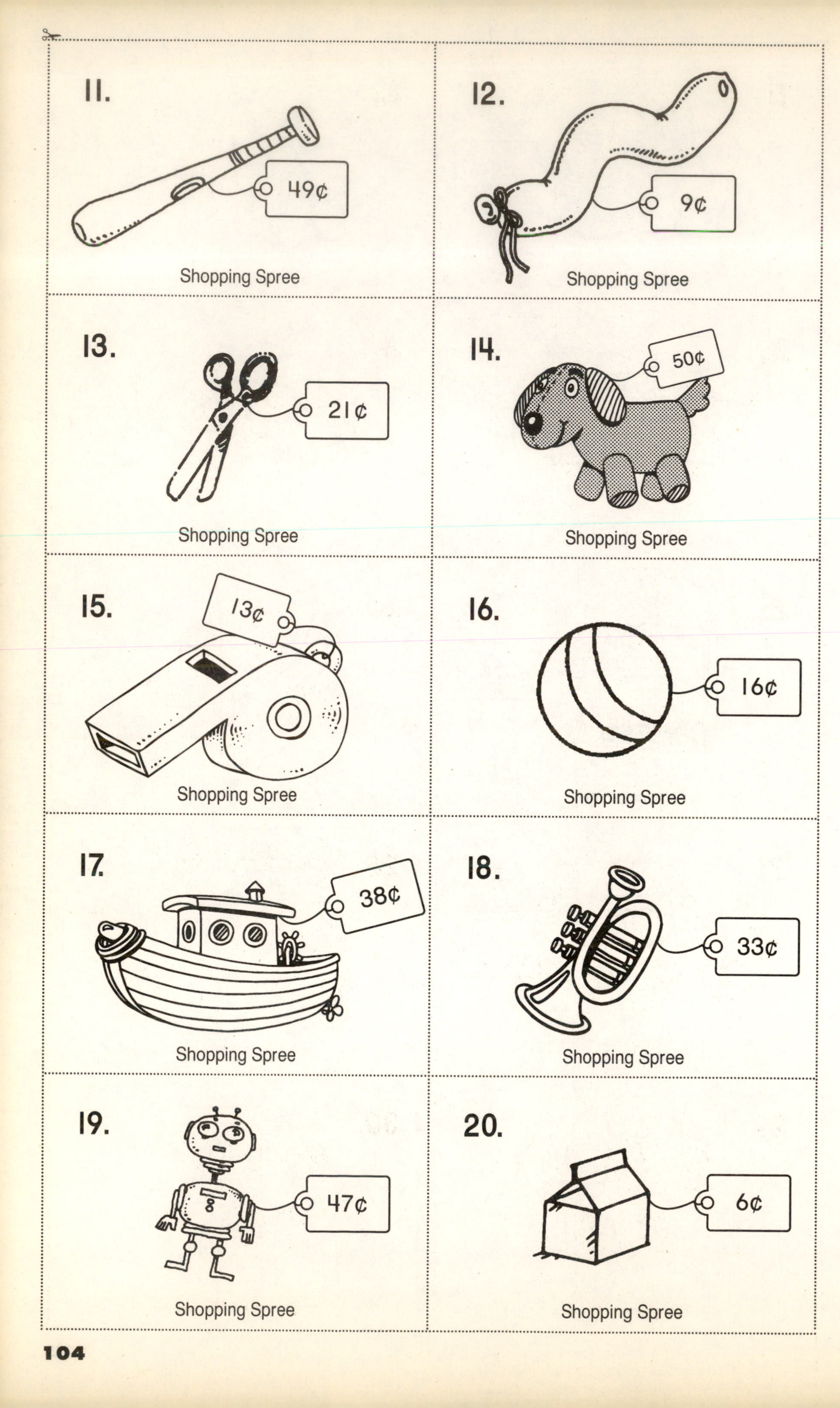
11.
49¢
Shopping Spree
12.
9¢
Shopping Spree
13.
21¢
Shopping Spree
14.
50¢
Shopping Spree
15.
13¢
Shopping Spree
16.
16¢
Shopping Spree
17.
38¢
Shopping Spree
18.
33¢
Shopping Spree
19.
47¢
Shopping Spree
20.
6¢
Shopping Spree

21.

Shopping Spree

22.

Shopping Spree

23.

Shopping Spree

24.

Shopping Spree

25.

Shopping Spree

26.

Shopping Spree

27.

Shopping Spree

28.

Shopping Spree

29.

Shopping Spree

30.

Shopping Spree

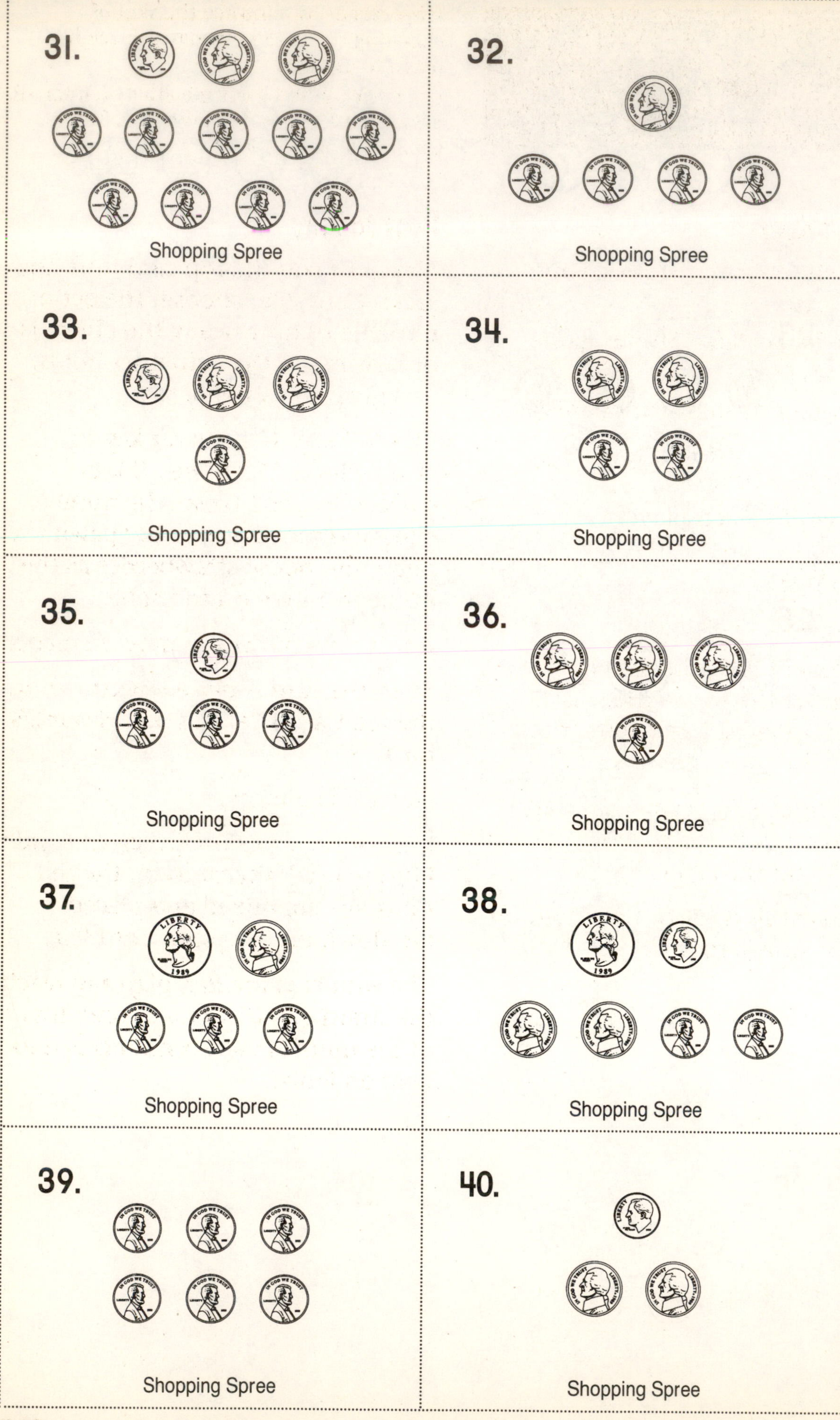
31.
Shopping Spree
32.
Shopping Spree
33.
Shopping Spree
34.
Shopping Spree
35.
Shopping Spree
36.
Shopping Spree
37.
Shopping Spree
38.
Shopping Spree
39.
Shopping Spree
40.
Shopping Spree

Strawberry Patch Stories

Objective: To reinforce the skill of choosing the better estimate of weight, mass, or capacity

Use with Grade 1 anytime after Chapter 10, Lesson 10-13; Grade 2, anytime after Chapter 9, Lesson 9-12

You Will Need

Strawberry Patch Stories game board

Strawberry Patch Stories game cards (36)

Strawberry Patch Stories answer key

1 number cube

1 pawn for each player

How to Start

Two or Three Players

Each player tosses the number cube. The player who tosses the least number is Player 1 and starts the game.

Player 2 mixes the game cards and places them facedown on the green Card Pile on the game board.

Each player puts his or her pawn on the Start strawberry.

How to Play

Player 1 takes the top card from the green Card Pile, chooses the better estimate of how heavy the object is or how much the container holds, and gives the answer.

Player 2 uses the answer key to check Player 1's answer. If it is correct, Player 1 tosses the number cube and moves his or her pawn the same number of strawberries as the number shown on the cube.

If it is not correct, no move is made.

Then the card is placed facedown in the red Card Pile, and it is Player 2's turn.

Players take turns.

If all of the cards on the green Card Pile are used, the cards on the red Card Pile are mixed and placed facedown on the green Card Pile.

The winner is the first player to reach the strawberry basket. An exact toss of the number cube is not needed to land on Finish.

Answer Key: Strawberry Patch Stories

1. more than 1 quart
2. less than 1 pint
3. less than 1 quart
4. more than 1 quart
5. more than 1 quart
6. less than 1 quart
7. less than 1 quart
8. more than 1 cup
9. more than 1 pint
10. more than 1 liter
11. less than 1 liter
12. more than 1 liter
13. less than 1 liter
14. less than 1 liter
15. more than 1 liter
16. more than 1 liter
17. less than 1 liter
18. less than 1 liter
19. less than 1 pound
20. more than 1 pound
21. less than 1 pound
22. more than 1 pound
23. more than 1 pound
24. less than 1 pound
25. more than 1 pound
26. more than 1 pound
27. less than 1 pound
28. more than 1 kilogram
29. less than 1 kilogram
30. less than 1 kilogram
31. less than 1 kilogram
32. less than 1 kilogram
33. more than 1 kilogram
34. less than 1 kilogram
35. less than 1 kilogram
36. more than 1 kilogram

1.

less than 1 gallon
more than 1 gallon

Strawberry Patch Stories

2.

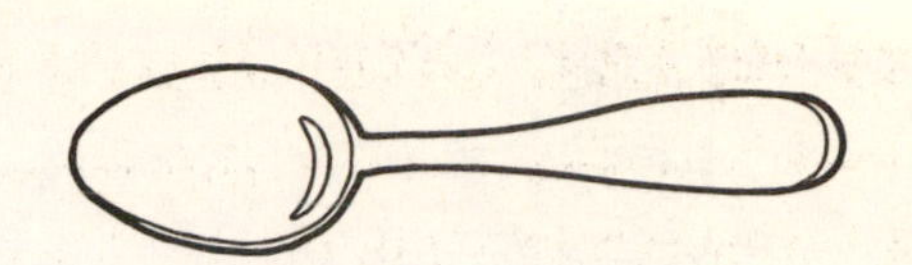

less than 1 pint
more than 1 pint

Strawberry Patch Stories

3.

less than 1 quart
more than 1 quart

Strawberry Patch Stories

4.

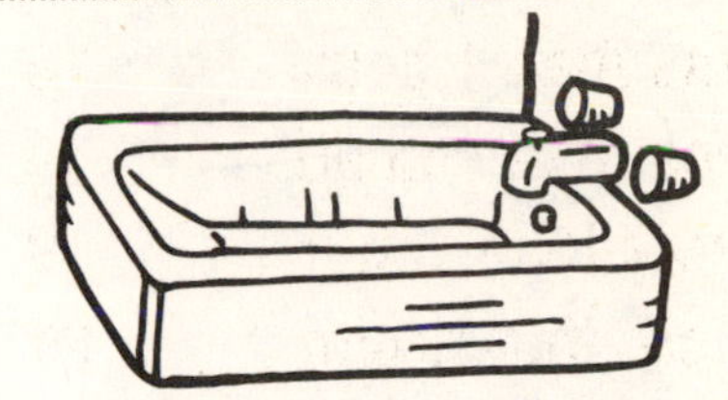

less than 1 gallon
more than 1 gallon

Strawberry Patch Stories

5.

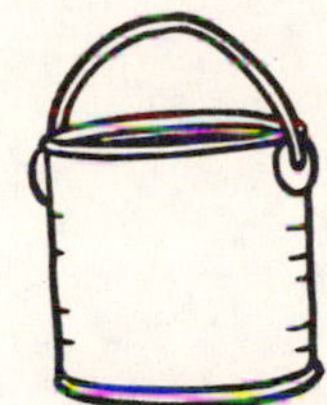

less than 1 quart
more than 1 quart

Strawberry Patch Stories

6.

less than 1 quart
more than 1 quart

Strawberry Patch Stories

7.

less than 1 quart
more than 1 quart

Strawberry Patch Stories

8.

less than 1 cup
more than 1 cup

Strawberry Patch Stories

9.

less than 1 pint
more than 1 pint

Strawberry Patch Stories

10.

less than 1 liter
more than 1 liter

Strawberry Patch Stories

11.

less than 1 liter
more than 1 liter

Strawberry Patch Stories

12.

less than 1 liter
more than 1 liter

Strawberry Patch Stories

13.

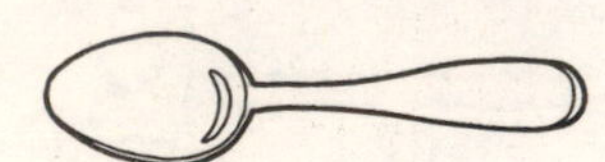

less than 1 liter
more than 1 liter

Strawberry Patch Stories

14.

less than 1 liter
more than 1 liter

Strawberry Patch Stories

15.

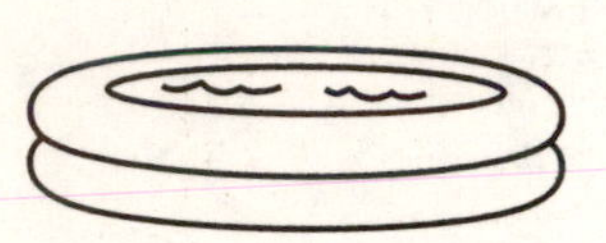

less than 1 liter
more than 1 liter

Strawberry Patch Stories

16.

less than 1 liter
more than 1 liter

Strawberry Patch Stories

17.

less than 1 liter
more than 1 liter

Strawberry Patch Stories

18.

less than 1 liter
more than 1 liter

Strawberry Patch Stories

19.

less than 1 pound
more than 1 pound

Strawberry Patch Stories

20.

less than 1 pound
more than 1 pound

Strawberry Patch Stories

21. 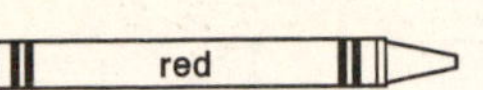

less than 1 pound
more than 1 pound

Strawberry Patch Stories

22. 

less than 1 pound
more than 1 pound

Strawberry Patch Stories

23. 

less than 1 pound
more than 1 pound

Strawberry Patch Stories

24. 

less than 1 pound
more than 1 pound

Strawberry Patch Stories

25. 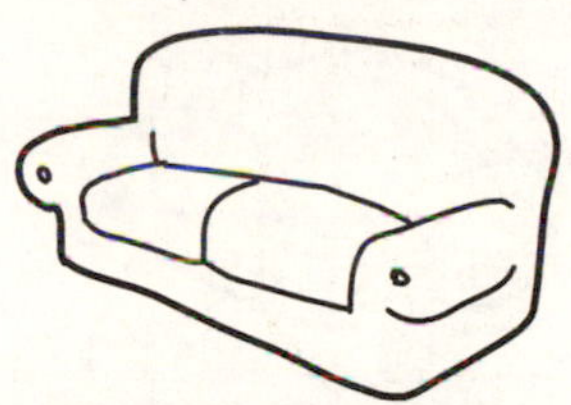

less than 1 pound
more than 1 pound

Strawberry Patch Stories

26. 

less than 1 pound
more than 1 pound

Strawberry Patch Stories

27. 

less than 1 pound
more than 1 pound

Strawberry Patch Stories

28. 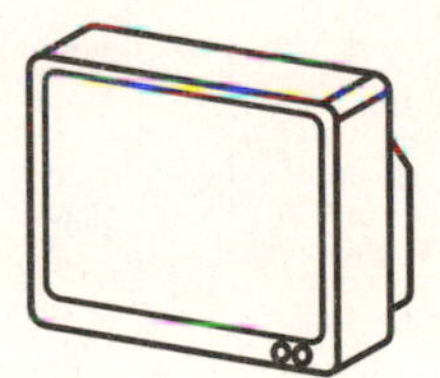

less than 1 kilogram
more than 1 kilogram

Strawberry Patch Stories

29. 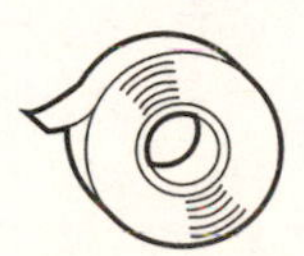

less than 1 kilogram
more than 1 kilogram

Strawberry Patch Stories

30. 

less than 1 kilogram
more than 1 kilogram

Strawberry Patch Stories

31. 

less than I kilogram
more than I kilogram

Strawberry Patch Stories

32. 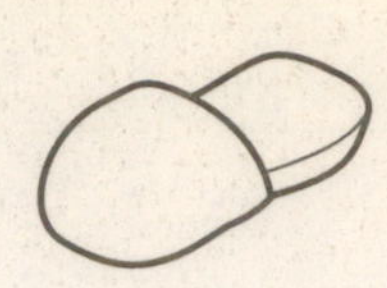

less than I kilogram
more than I kilogram

Strawberry Patch Stories

33. 

less than I kilogram
more than I kilogram

Strawberry Patch Stories

34. 

less than I kilogram
more than I kilogram

Strawberry Patch Stories

35. 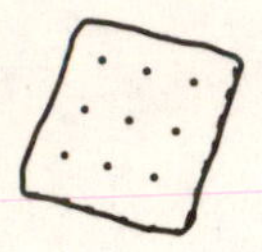

less than I kilogram
more than I kilogram

Strawberry Patch Stories

36. 

less than I kilogram
more than I kilogram

Strawberry Patch Stories

All Aboard

Objective: To reinforce the skill of finding sums and differences for numbers through 18

Use with Grade 1 anytime after Chapter 11, Lesson 11-12; Grade 2, anytime after Chapter 2, Lesson 2-10

You Will Need

All Aboard game board

All Aboard game cards (36)

All Aboard answer key
or counters (18 for each player)

1 number cube

1 pawn for each player

How to Start

Two or Three Players

Each player tosses the number cube. The player who tosses the greatest number is Player 1 and starts the game.

Player 2 mixes the game cards and places them facedown on the green Card Pile on the game board.

Each player puts his or her pawn on the Hop Aboard space.

How to Play

Player 1 takes the top card from the green Card Pile, adds or subtracts, and gives the answer.

Player 2 uses the answer key or counters to check Player 1's answer. If it is correct, Player 1 tosses the number cube and moves his or her pawn the same number of spaces along the railroad tracks as the number shown on the cube.

If it is not correct, no move is made.

Then the card is placed on the red Card Pile, and it is Player 2's turn.

Players take turns. If all of the cards in the green Card Pile are used, the cards in the red Card Pile are mixed and placed facedown on the green Card Pile.

The winner is the first player to reach the end of the railroad line. An exact toss of the cube is not needed to reach Finish.

Answer Key: All Aboard

1.	11	13.	9	25.	13
2.	12	14.	14	26.	10
3.	8	15.	8	27.	10
4.	6	16.	10	28.	12
5.	11	17.	14	29.	11
6.	16	18.	6	30.	4
7.	8	19.	14	31.	9
8.	13	20.	12	32.	3
9.	9	21.	9	33.	7
10.	5	22.	9	34.	10
11.	9	23.	5	35.	12
12.	13	24.	7	36.	6

9.	7.	5.	3.	1.
$17 - 8 =$ ___	$5 + 3 =$ ___	$4 + 7 =$ ___	$11 - 3 =$ ___	$5 + 6 =$ ___
All Aboard	All Aboard	All Aboard	All Aboard	All Aboard
10.	**8.**	**6.**	**4.**	**2.**
$12 - 7 =$ ___	$9 + 4 =$ ___	$8 + 8 =$ ___	$12 - 6 =$ ___	$8 + 4 =$ ___
All Aboard	All Aboard	All Aboard	All Aboard	All Aboard

11.

$$\begin{array}{r} 2 \\ +7 \\ \hline \end{array}$$

All Aboard

12.

$$\begin{array}{r} 8 \\ +5 \\ \hline \end{array}$$

All Aboard

13.

$$\begin{array}{r} 4 \\ +5 \\ \hline \end{array}$$

All Aboard

14.

$$\begin{array}{r} 7 \\ +7 \\ \hline \end{array}$$

All Aboard

15.

$$\begin{array}{r} 16 \\ -\ 8 \\ \hline \end{array}$$

All Aboard

16.

$$\begin{array}{r} 3 \\ +7 \\ \hline \end{array}$$

All Aboard

17.

$$\begin{array}{r} 8 \\ +6 \\ \hline \end{array}$$

All Aboard

18.

$$\begin{array}{r} 13 \\ -\ 7 \\ \hline \end{array}$$

All Aboard

19.

$$\begin{array}{r} 9 \\ +5 \\ \hline \end{array}$$

All Aboard

20.

$$\begin{array}{r} 3 \\ +9 \\ \hline \end{array}$$

All Aboard

29.

$$\begin{array}{r} 2 \\ +9 \\ \hline \end{array}$$

All Aboard

27.

$$\begin{array}{r} 1 \\ +9 \\ \hline \end{array}$$

All Aboard

25.

$$\begin{array}{r} 6 \\ +7 \\ \hline \end{array}$$

All Aboard

23.

$$\begin{array}{r} 13 \\ -\ 8 \\ \hline \end{array}$$

All Aboard

21.

$$\begin{array}{r} 14 \\ -\ 5 \\ \hline \end{array}$$

All Aboard

30.

$$\begin{array}{r} 13 \\ -\ 9 \\ \hline \end{array}$$

All Aboard

28.

$$\begin{array}{r} 7 \\ +5 \\ \hline \end{array}$$

All Aboard

26.

$$\begin{array}{r} 8 \\ +2 \\ \hline \end{array}$$

All Aboard

24.

$$\begin{array}{r} 12 \\ -\ 5 \\ \hline \end{array}$$

All Aboard

22.

$$\begin{array}{r} 18 \\ -\ 9 \\ \hline \end{array}$$

All Aboard

31.

$$\begin{array}{r} 16 \\ -\ 7 \\ \hline \end{array}$$

All Aboard

32.

$$\begin{array}{r} 11 \\ -\ 8 \\ \hline \end{array}$$

All Aboard

33.

$$\begin{array}{r} 14 \\ -\ 7 \\ \hline \end{array}$$

All Aboard

34.

$$\begin{array}{r} 5 \\ +5 \\ \hline \end{array}$$

All Aboard

35.

$$\begin{array}{r} 6 \\ +6 \\ \hline \end{array}$$

All Aboard

36.

$$\begin{array}{r} 10 \\ -\ 4 \\ \hline \end{array}$$

All Aboard

Deep-Sea Diver

Objective: To reinforce the skill of adding or subtracting with two-digit numbers

Use with Grade 1 anytime after Chapter 12, Lesson 12-8; Grade 2, anytime after Chapter 4, Lesson 4-6

You Will Need

Deep-Sea Diver game board

Deep-Sea Diver game cards (18)

Teacher's Note: You will need to cut on the dotted lines, fold on the solid fold lines, and paste the front and back sides of the cards together for this game.

Deep-Sea Diver answer key *or* counters (9 each of 10-unit and 1-unit for each player)

1 number cube

Scratch paper and pencils

How to Start

Two Players

Each player tosses the number cube. The player who tosses the lesser number is Player 1 and starts the game.

Player 2 mixes the game cards and places them facedown on the green Card Pile on the game board.

Players use scratch paper and pencils to solve the problems.

How to Play

Player 1 takes the top card from the card pile, adds or subtracts, and gives the answer.

Player 2 uses the answer key or counters to check Player 1's answer. If it is correct, Player 1 places the card on the same answer on the diver's grid picture side up.

If it is not correct, the card is placed facedown at the bottom of the Card Pile.

Players take turns.

The winner is the player who places the last card on the diver's grid to complete the picture.

Answer Key: Deep-Sea Diver

1. 79	7. 77	13. 66
2. 61	8. 65	14. 76
3. 99	9. 48	15. 11
4. 78	10. 32	16. 42
5. 36	11. 59	17. 87
6. 72	12. 98	18. 50

Variation

This game may be played by one player as an independent activity. The player takes a card, solves the problem, checks the answer, and puts together the picture.

FOLD

1.

tens	ones
5	8
+2	1

Deep-Sea Diver

2.

tens	ones
7	4
−1	3

Deep-Sea Diver

3.

tens	ones
2	5
+7	4

Deep-Sea Diver

4.

tens	ones
1	8
+6	0

Deep-Sea Diver

5.

tens	ones
4	9
−1	3

Deep-Sea Diver

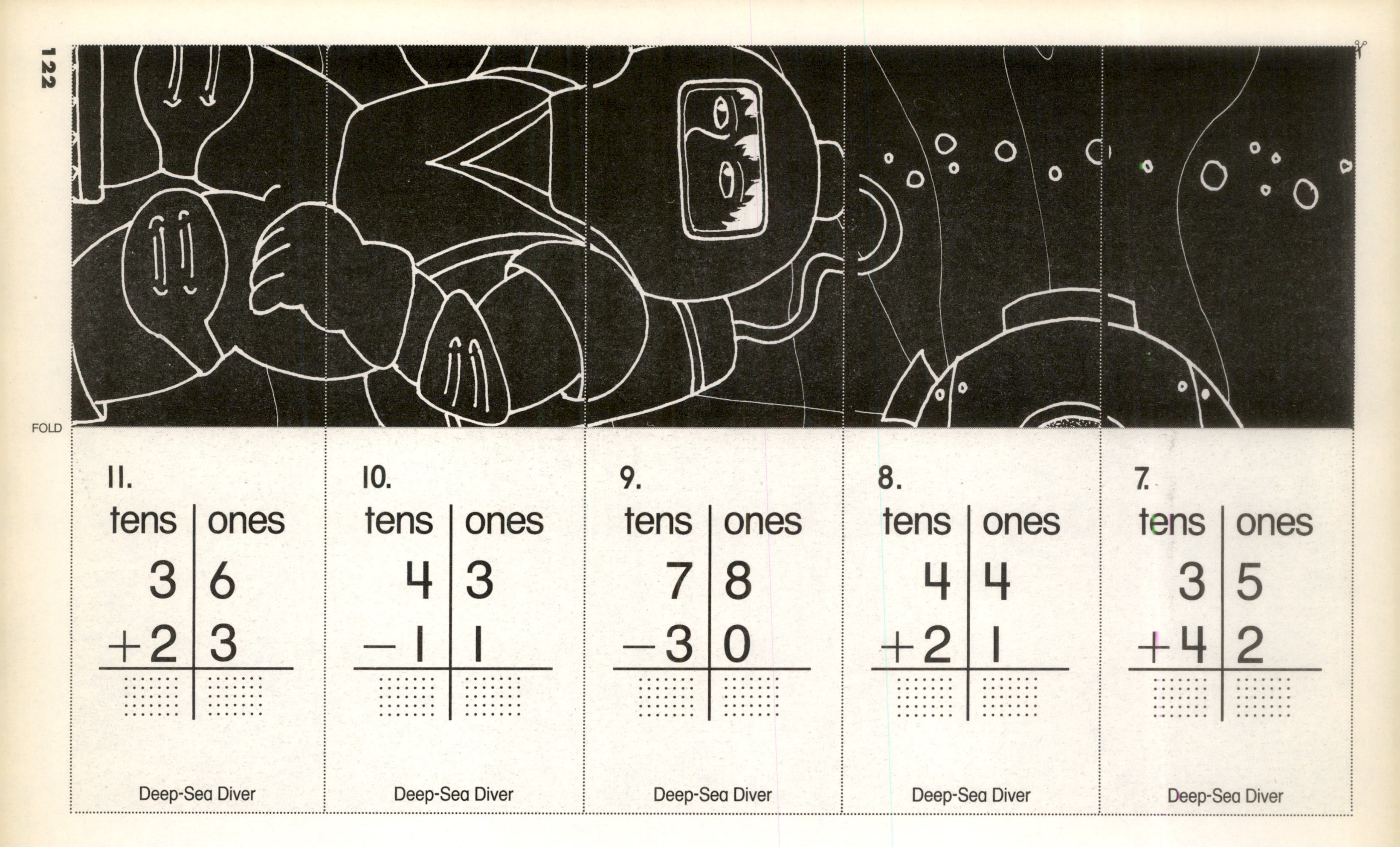

FOLD

11.

tens	ones
3	6
+2	3

Deep-Sea Diver

10.

tens	ones
4	3
−1	1

Deep-Sea Diver

9.

tens	ones
7	8
−3	0

Deep-Sea Diver

8.

tens	ones
4	4
+2	1

Deep-Sea Diver

7.

tens	ones
3	5
+4	2

Deep-Sea Diver

FOLD

13.

	tens	ones
	6	1
+		5

Deep-Sea Diver

14.

	tens	ones
		4
+	7	2

Deep-Sea Diver

15.

	tens	ones
	1	3
−		2

Deep-Sea Diver

16.

	tens	ones
	6	8
−	2	6

Deep-Sea Diver

17.

	tens	ones
		3
+	8	4

Deep-Sea Diver

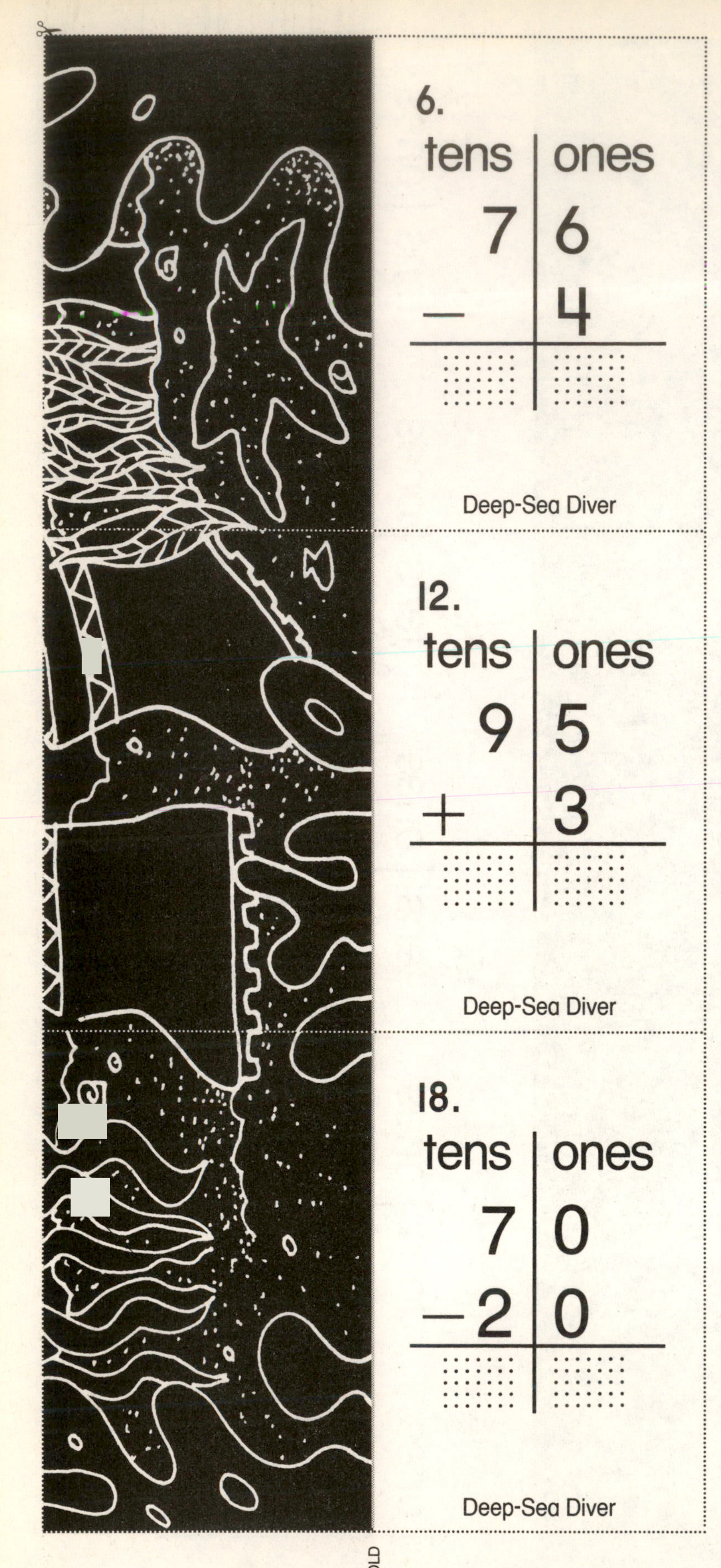

6.

tens	ones
7	6
−	4

Deep-Sea Diver

12.

tens	ones
9	5
+	3

Deep-Sea Diver

18.

tens	ones
7	0
− 2	0

Deep-Sea Diver

FOLD

Farmer's Market

Objective: To reinforce the skill of adding two-digit numbers, with and without regrouping

Use with Grade 2 anytime after Chapter 5, Lesson 5-4

You Will Need

Farmer's Market game board

Farmer's Market game cards (18)

Teacher's Note: You will need to cut on the dotted lines, fold on the solid fold lines, and paste the front and back sides of the cards together for this game.

Farmer's Market answer key *or* counters (9 each of 10-unit and 1-unit for each player)

1 number cube

Scratch paper and pencils

How to Start

Two Players

Each player tosses the number cube. The player who tosses the greater number is Player 1 and starts the game.

Player 2 mixes the game cards and places them facedown on the green Card Pile on the game board.

Players use scratch paper and pencils to solve the problems.

How to Play

Player 1 takes the top card from the green Card Pile, finds the sum, and gives the answer.

Player 2 uses the answer key or counters to check Player 1's answer. If it is correct, Player 1 places the card on the same answer on the vegetable grid picture side up.

If it is not correct, the card is placed on the red Card Pile.

Then it is Player 2's turn.

Players take turns. If all of the cards on the green Card Pile are used, the cards on the red Card Pile are mixed and placed facedown on the green Card Pile.

The winner is the player who puts the last card on the vegetable grid to complete the picture.

Answer Key: Farmer's Market		
1. 63	7. 86	13. 34
2. 71	8. 62	14. 50
3. 65	9. 90	15. 70
4. 60	10. 93	16. 58
5. 91	11. 92	17. 82
6. 88	12. 64	18. 84

Variation

Farmer's Market can be played by one player as an individual activity. The player takes a game card, solves the problem, checks the answer, and puts the picture together.

1.

$$\begin{array}{r} 47 \\ +\ 16 \\ \hline \end{array}$$

Farmer's Market

2.

$$\begin{array}{r} 26 \\ +\ 45 \\ \hline \end{array}$$

Farmer's Market

3.

$$\begin{array}{r} 38 \\ +\ 27 \\ \hline \end{array}$$

Farmer's Market

4.

$$\begin{array}{r} 29 \\ +\ 31 \\ \hline \end{array}$$

Farmer's Market

5.

$$\begin{array}{r} 73 \\ +\ 18 \\ \hline \end{array}$$

Farmer's Market

FOLD

7.

$$\begin{array}{r} 61 \\ +\ 25 \\ \hline \end{array}$$

Farmer's Market

8.

$$\begin{array}{r} 27 \\ +\ 35 \\ \hline \end{array}$$

Farmer's Market

9.

$$\begin{array}{r} 52 \\ +\ 38 \\ \hline \end{array}$$

Farmer's Market

10.

$$\begin{array}{r} 78 \\ +\ 15 \\ \hline \end{array}$$

Farmer's Market

11.

$$\begin{array}{r} 64 \\ +\ 28 \\ \hline \end{array}$$

Farmer's Market

FOLD

13.

$$\begin{array}{r} 17 \\ +\ 17 \\ \hline \end{array}$$

Farmer's Market

14.

$$\begin{array}{r} 32 \\ +\ 18 \\ \hline \end{array}$$

Farmer's Market

15.

$$\begin{array}{r} 43 \\ +\ 27 \\ \hline \end{array}$$

Farmer's Market

16.

$$\begin{array}{r} 36 \\ +\ 22 \\ \hline \end{array}$$

Farmer's Market

17.

$$\begin{array}{r} 46 \\ +\ 36 \\ \hline \end{array}$$

Farmer's Market

FOLD

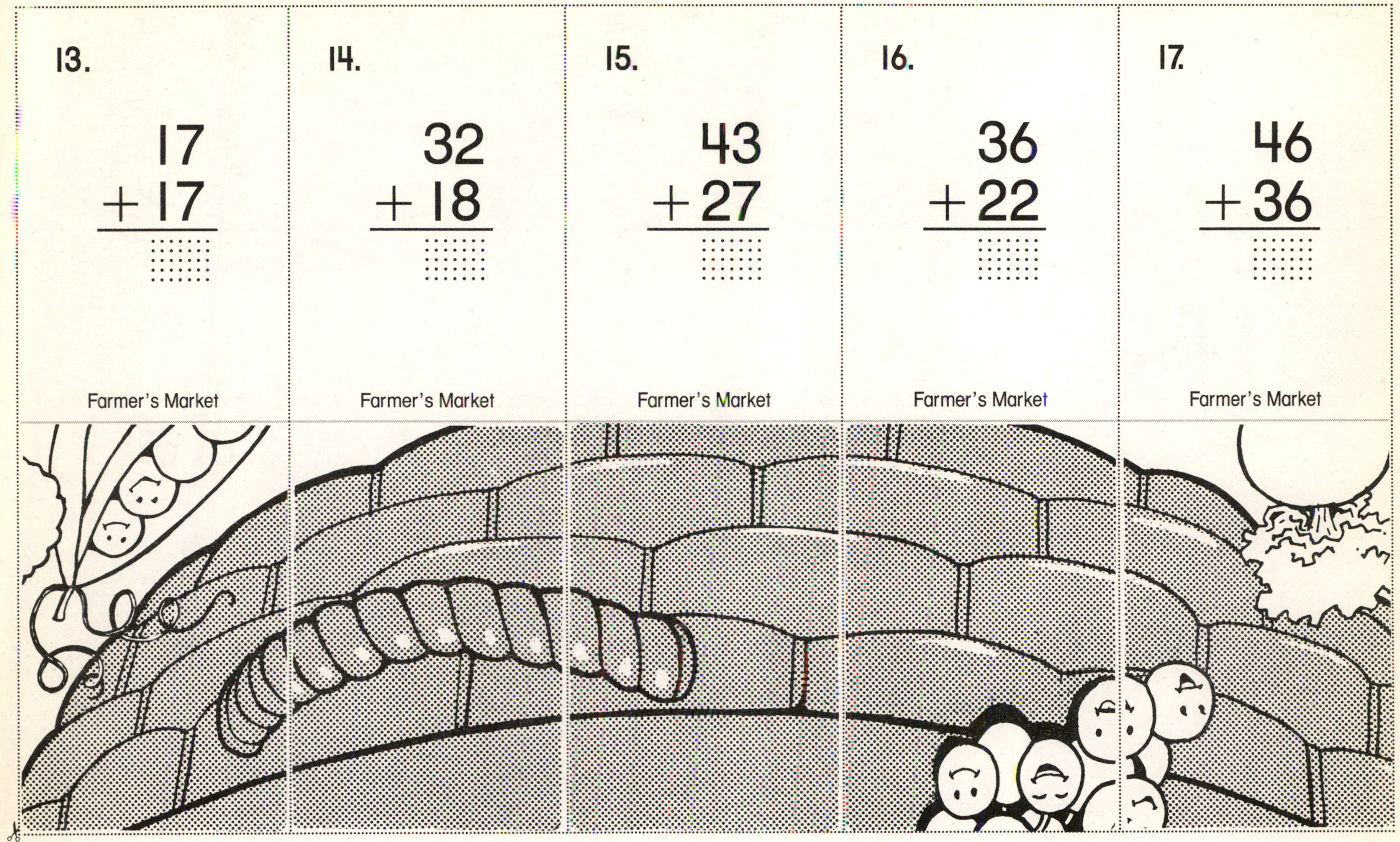

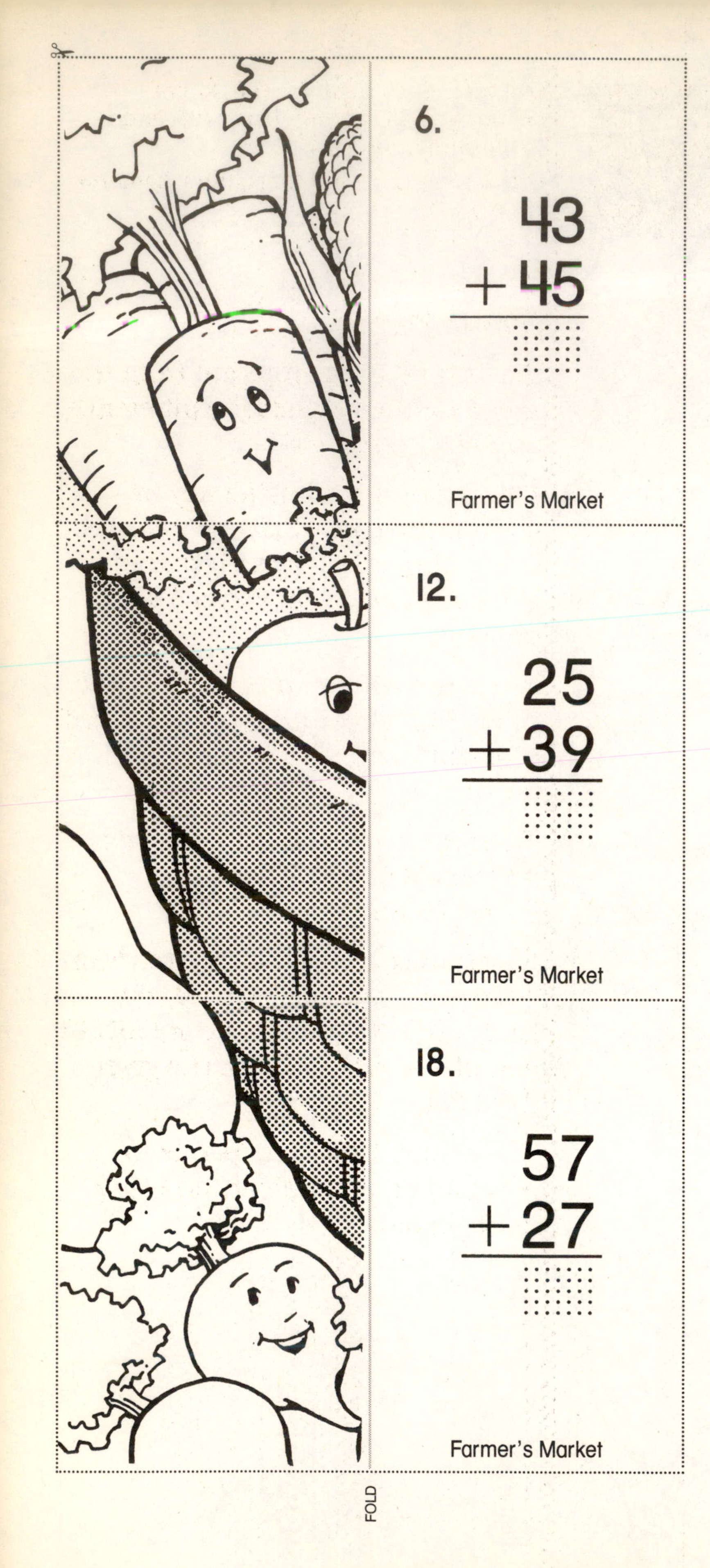

6.

$$\begin{array}{r} 43 \\ +\,45 \\ \hline \end{array}$$

Farmer's Market

12.

$$\begin{array}{r} 25 \\ +\,39 \\ \hline \end{array}$$

Farmer's Market

18.

$$\begin{array}{r} 57 \\ +\,27 \\ \hline \end{array}$$

Farmer's Market

FOLD

Subzero Subtraction

Objective: To reinforce the skill of subtracting 2-digit numbers, with and without regrouping

Use with Grade 2 anytime after Chapter 6, Lesson 6-4.

You Will Need

Subzero Subtraction game board

Subzero Subtraction game cards (36)

Subzero Subtraction answer key *or* counters (9 of 10-unit and 15 of 1-unit for each player)

20 round markers in 2 colors (10 of each color)

1 number cube

How to Start

Two Players

Each player tosses the number cube. The player who tosses the lesser number is Player 1 and starts the game.

Player 2 mixes the cards and places them facedown on the green Card Pile on the game board.

Each player starts with 10 round markers of 1 color.

How to Play

Player 1 takes the top card from the green Card Pile, finds the difference, and gives the answer.

Player 2 uses the answer key or counters to check Player 1's answer. If it is correct, a marker is placed on the same answer on Player 1's penguin.

If it is not correct, no marker is put down. If it already has been covered or is not there, no marker is put down.

Then the card is placed facedown on the red Card Pile, and it is Player 2's turn.

Players take turns. If all the cards on the green Card Pile are used, the cards on the red Card Pile are mixed and placed facedown on the green Card Pile.

The winner is the first player to cover all of the numbers on his or her penguin.

Answer Key: Subzero Subtraction

1. 19
2. 24
3. 42
4. 5
5. 19
6. 17
7. 47
8. 18
9. 9
10. 33
11. 28
12. 12
13. 18
14. 39
15. 25
16. 16
17. 39
18. 24
19. 45
20. 12
21. 17
22. 29
23. 26
24. 38
25. 9
26. 26
27. 33
28. 40
29. 4
30. 35
31. 28
32. 13
33. 29
34. 25
35. 50
36. 67

Variation

Players can check their own subtraction answers by adding.

1.

$$\begin{array}{r} 34 \\ -\ 15 \\ \hline \end{array}$$

Subzero Subtraction

2.

$$\begin{array}{r} 66 \\ -\ 42 \\ \hline \end{array}$$

Subzero Subtraction

3.

$$\begin{array}{r} 81 \\ -\ 39 \\ \hline \end{array}$$

Subzero Subtraction

4.

$$\begin{array}{r} 21 \\ -\ 16 \\ \hline \end{array}$$

Subzero Subtraction

5.

$$\begin{array}{r} 48 \\ -\ 29 \\ \hline \end{array}$$

Subzero Subtraction

6.

$$\begin{array}{r} 71 \\ -\ 54 \\ \hline \end{array}$$

Subzero Subtraction

7.

$$\begin{array}{r} 82 \\ -\ 35 \\ \hline \end{array}$$

Subzero Subtraction

8.

$$\begin{array}{r} 63 \\ -\ 45 \\ \hline \end{array}$$

Subzero Subtraction

9.

$$\begin{array}{r} 26 \\ -\ 17 \\ \hline \end{array}$$

Subzero Subtraction

10.

$$\begin{array}{r} 84 \\ -\ 51 \\ \hline \end{array}$$

Subzero Subtraction

11.

$$\begin{array}{r} 92 \\ -\ 64 \\ \hline \end{array}$$

Subzero Subtraction

12.

$$\begin{array}{r} 83 \\ -\ 71 \\ \hline \end{array}$$

Subzero Subtraction

13.

$$\begin{array}{r} 36 \\ -\ 18 \\ \hline \end{array}$$

Subzero Subtraction

14.

$$\begin{array}{r} 77 \\ -\ 38 \\ \hline \end{array}$$

Subzero Subtraction

15.

$$\begin{array}{r} 52 \\ -\ 27 \\ \hline \end{array}$$

Subzero Subtraction

16.

$$\begin{array}{r} 33 \\ -\ 17 \\ \hline \end{array}$$

Subzero Subtraction

17.

$$\begin{array}{r} 64 \\ -\ 25 \\ \hline \end{array}$$

Subzero Subtraction

18.

$$\begin{array}{r} 38 \\ -\ 14 \\ \hline \end{array}$$

Subzero Subtraction

19.

$$\begin{array}{r} 73 \\ -\ 28 \\ \hline \end{array}$$

Subzero Subtraction

20.

$$\begin{array}{r} 48 \\ -\ 36 \\ \hline \end{array}$$

Subzero Subtraction

21.

$$\begin{array}{r} 33 \\ -\ 16 \\ \hline \end{array}$$

Subzero Subtraction

22.

$$\begin{array}{r} 73 \\ -\ 44 \\ \hline \end{array}$$

Subzero Subtraction

23.

$$\begin{array}{r} 51 \\ -\ 25 \\ \hline \end{array}$$

Subzero Subtraction

24.

$$\begin{array}{r} 87 \\ -\ 49 \\ \hline \end{array}$$

Subzero Subtraction

25.

$$\begin{array}{r} 25 \\ -\ 16 \\ \hline \end{array}$$

Subzero Subtraction

26.

$$\begin{array}{r} 43 \\ -\ 17 \\ \hline \end{array}$$

Subzero Subtraction

27.

$$\begin{array}{r} 58 \\ -\ 25 \\ \hline \end{array}$$

Subzero Subtraction

28.

$$\begin{array}{r} 76 \\ -\ 36 \\ \hline \end{array}$$

Subzero Subtraction

29.

$$\begin{array}{r} 42 \\ -\ 38 \\ \hline \end{array}$$

Subzero Subtraction

30.

$$\begin{array}{r} 62 \\ -\ 27 \\ \hline \end{array}$$

Subzero Subtraction

35.	33.	31.
$75 - 25$	$88 - 59$	$44 - 16$
Subzero Subtraction	Subzero Subtraction	Subzero Subtraction
36.	34.	32.
$84 - 17$	$51 - 26$	$91 - 78$
Subzero Subtraction	Subzero Subtraction	Subzero Subtraction

Tic, Tac, Snow!

Objective: To reinforce the skill of ordering numbers through 999

Use with Grade 2 anytime after Chapter 10, Lesson 10-8.

You Will Need

Tic, Tac, Snow! game board

Tic, Tac, Snow! game cards (36)

Tic, Tac, Snow! answer key
or counters (9 each of 100-unit, 10 unit, and 1-unit for each player)

18 round markers in 2 colors (9 of each color)

1 number cube

How to Start

Two Players

Each player tosses the number cube. The player who tosses the greater number is Player 1 and starts the game.

Player 2 mixes the game cards and places them facedown on the green Card Pile on the game board.

Each player starts with 9 round markers of 1 color.

How to Play

Tic, Tac, Snow! is played like tic-tac-toe.

Player 1 takes the top card from the green Card Pile, finds the missing number, and gives the answer.

Player 2 uses the answer key or counters to check Player 1's answer. If it is correct, a marker is placed on the same answer on Player 1's snowman.

If it is not correct, no marker is put down. If it already has been covered or is not there, no marker is put down.

Then the card is placed on the red Card Pile, and it is Player 2's turn.

Players take turns. If all of the cards on the green Card Pile are used, the cards in the red Card Pile are mixed and placed facedown on the green Card Pile.

The winner is the first player to put three markers across, down, or diagonally on his or her snowman.

Answer Key: Tic, Tac, Snow!

1. 633	13. 221	25. 231
2. 601	14. 710	26. 667
3. 898	15. 557	27. 980
4. 422	16. 667	28. 221
5. 501	17. 721	29. 231
6. 408	18. 601	30. 710
7. 115	19. 898	31. 477
8. 369	20. 236	32. 633
9. 980	21. 369	33. 106
10. 106	22. 557	34. 501
11. 236	23. 408	35. 422
12. 477	24. 115	36. 721

Variation

A player can put his or her markers on either snowman. The first player to place three markers across, down, or diagonally on either snowman is the winner. Players can use number charts that show numbers 0–999 as answer keys.

1. ______, 634, 635 Tic, Tac, Snow!	2. 600, ______, 602 Tic, Tac, Snow!
3. 896, 897, ______ Tic, Tac, Snow!	4. ______, 423, 424 Tic, Tac, Snow!
5. 500, ______, 502 Tic, Tac, Snow!	6. 406, 407, ______ Tic, Tac, Snow!
7. ______, 116, 117 Tic, Tac, Snow!	8. 368, ______, 370 Tic, Tac, Snow!
9. 978, 979, ______ Tic, Tac, Snow!	10. ______, 107, 108 Tic, Tac, Snow!

11.

235, ____, 237

Tic, Tac, Snow!

12.

475, 476, ____

Tic, Tac, Snow!

13.

____, 222, 223

Tic, Tac, Snow!

14.

708, 709, ____

Tic, Tac, Snow!

15.

555, 556, ____

Tic, Tac, Snow!

16.

666, ____, 668

Tic, Tac, Snow!

17.

720, ____, 722

Tic, Tac, Snow!

18.

____, 602, 603

Tic, Tac, Snow!

19.

____, 899, 900

Tic, Tac, Snow!

20.

234, 235, ____

Tic, Tac, Snow!

21.

____, 370, 371

Tic, Tac, Snow!

22.

____, 558, 559

Tic, Tac, Snow!

23.

____, 409, 410

Tic, Tac, Snow!

24.

113, 114, ____

Tic, Tac, Snow!

25.

229, 230, ____

Tic, Tac, Snow!

26.

____, 668, 669

Tic, Tac, Snow!

27.

____, 981, 982

Tic, Tac, Snow!

28.

220, ____, 222

Tic, Tac, Snow!

29.

____, 232, 233

Tic, Tac, Snow!

30.

709, ____, 711

Tic, Tac, Snow!

31.

______, 478, 479

Tic, Tac, Snow!

32.

631, 632, ______

Tic, Tac, Snow!

33.

105, ______, 107

Tic, Tac, Snow!

34.

499, 500, ______

Tic, Tac, Snow!

35.

421, ______, 423

Tic, Tac, Snow!

36.

______, 722, 723

Tic, Tac, Snow!

Gift Boxes

Objective: To reinforce the skill of adding and subtracting amounts of money

Use with Grade 2 anytime after Chapter 11, Enrichment, p. 459.

You Will Need

Gift Boxes game board

Gift Boxes game cards

Gift Boxes answer key
or counters (9 of 100-unit, 9 of 10-unit, and 9 of 1-unit for each player)

1 number cube

18 round markers in 2 colors (9 of each color)

Scratch paper and pencils

How to Start

Two Players

Each player tosses the number cube. The player who tosses the greater number is Player 1 and starts the game.

Player 2 mixes the cards and places them facedown on the green Card Pile on the game board.

Each player starts with 9 round markers of 1 color.

Players use scratch paper and pencils to solve the problems.

How to Play

Gift Boxes is played like tic-tac-toe.

Player 1 takes the top card from the green Card Pile, adds or subtracts the numbers, and gives the answer.

Player 2 uses the answer key or counters to check Player 1's answer. If it is correct, a marker is placed on the same answer on Player 1's gift box.

If it is not correct, no marker is put down. If it already has been covered or it is not there, no marker is put down.

Then the card is placed on the red Card Pile, and it is Player 2's turn.

If all of the cards on the green Card Pile are used, the cards on the red Card Pile are mixed and placed facedown on the green Card Pile.

The winner is the first player to put three markers across, down, or diagonally on his or her gift box.

Answer Key: Gift Boxes

1. $7.57	13. $2.15	25. $9.69
2. $9.90	14. $6.42	26. $3.54
3. $4.54	15. $6.48	27. $7.94
4. $7.94	16. $9.69	28. $3.70
5. $1.71	17. $6.42	29. $8.90
6. $2.15	18. $2.37	30. $6.18
7. $3.70	19. $5.54	31. $5.54
8. $6.90	20. $2.25	32. $8.65
9. $2.05	21. $9.08	33. $2.15
10. $9.09	22. $6.42	34. $8.90
11. $3.70	23. $7.75	35. $6.90
12. $9.07	24. $2.71	36. $9.36

Variation

Players can put their markers on either gift box. The first player to place three markers across, down, or diagonally on either gift box is the winner.

1.

$$\begin{array}{r} \$9.29 \\ -\ 1.72 \\ \hline \end{array}$$

Gift Boxes

2.

$$\begin{array}{r} \$8.21 \\ +\ 1.69 \\ \hline \end{array}$$

Gift Boxes

3.

$$\begin{array}{r} \$9.64 \\ -\ 5.10 \\ \hline \end{array}$$

Gift Boxes

4.

$$\begin{array}{r} \$4.88 \\ +\ 3.06 \\ \hline \end{array}$$

Gift Boxes

5.

$$\begin{array}{r} \$9.27 \\ -\ 7.56 \\ \hline \end{array}$$

Gift Boxes

6.

$$\begin{array}{r} \$1.53 \\ +\ 0.62 \\ \hline \end{array}$$

Gift Boxes

7.

$$\begin{array}{r} \$8.23 \\ -\ 4.53 \\ \hline \end{array}$$

Gift Boxes

8.

$$\begin{array}{r} \$3.89 \\ +\ 3.01 \\ \hline \end{array}$$

Gift Boxes

9.

$$\begin{array}{r} \$7.51 \\ -\ 5.46 \\ \hline \end{array}$$

Gift Boxes

10.

$$\begin{array}{r} \$6.82 \\ +\ 2.27 \\ \hline \end{array}$$

Gift Boxes

11.

$$\begin{array}{r} \$5.06 \\ -\ 1.36 \\ \hline \end{array}$$

Gift Boxes

12.

$$\begin{array}{r} \$4.44 \\ +\ 4.63 \\ \hline \end{array}$$

Gift Boxes

13.

$$\begin{array}{r} \$9.43 \\ -\ 7.28 \\ \hline \end{array}$$

Gift Boxes

14.

$$\begin{array}{r} \$5.11 \\ +\ 1.31 \\ \hline \end{array}$$

Gift Boxes

15.

$$\begin{array}{r} \$8.57 \\ -\ 2.09 \\ \hline \end{array}$$

Gift Boxes

16.

$$\begin{array}{r} \$5.87 \\ +\ 3.82 \\ \hline \end{array}$$

Gift Boxes

17.

$$\begin{array}{r} \$9.13 \\ -\ 2.71 \\ \hline \end{array}$$

Gift Boxes

18.

$$\begin{array}{r} \$1.94 \\ +\ 0.43 \\ \hline \end{array}$$

Gift Boxes

19.

$$\begin{array}{r} \$2.60 \\ +\ 2.94 \\ \hline \end{array}$$

Gift Boxes

20.

$$\begin{array}{r} \$9.60 \\ -\ 7.35 \\ \hline \end{array}$$

Gift Boxes

21.

$$\begin{array}{r} \$8.34 \\ +\ 0.74 \\ \hline \end{array}$$

Gift Boxes

22.

$$\begin{array}{r} \$8.75 \\ -\ 2.33 \\ \hline \end{array}$$

Gift Boxes

23.

$$\begin{array}{r} \$4.36 \\ +\ 3.39 \\ \hline \end{array}$$

Gift Boxes

24.

$$\begin{array}{r} \$7.07 \\ -\ 4.36 \\ \hline \end{array}$$

Gift Boxes

25.

$$\begin{array}{r} \$7.87 \\ +\ 1.82 \\ \hline \end{array}$$

Gift Boxes

26.

$$\begin{array}{r} \$8.35 \\ -\ 4.81 \\ \hline \end{array}$$

Gift Boxes

27.

$$\begin{array}{r} \$5.09 \\ +\ 2.85 \\ \hline \end{array}$$

Gift Boxes

28.

$$\begin{array}{r} \$8.00 \\ -\ 4.30 \\ \hline \end{array}$$

Gift Boxes

29.

$$\begin{array}{r} \$3.66 \\ +\ 5.24 \\ \hline \end{array}$$

Gift Boxes

30.

$$\begin{array}{r} \$9.50 \\ -\ 3.32 \\ \hline \end{array}$$

Gift Boxes

31.

$$\begin{array}{r} \$8.71 \\ -\ 3.17 \\ \hline \end{array}$$

Gift Boxes

32.

$$\begin{array}{r} \$2.40 \\ +\ 6.25 \\ \hline \end{array}$$

Gift Boxes

33.

$$\begin{array}{r} \$4.21 \\ -\ 2.06 \\ \hline \end{array}$$

Gift Boxes

34.

$$\begin{array}{r} \$5.22 \\ +\ 3.68 \\ \hline \end{array}$$

Gift Boxes

35.

$$\begin{array}{r} \$9.25 \\ -\ 2.35 \\ \hline \end{array}$$

Gift Boxes

36.

$$\begin{array}{r} \$3.61 \\ +\ 5.75 \\ \hline \end{array}$$

Gift Boxes

Shell Facts

Objective: To reinforce the skills of adding or multiplying objects in equal groups

Use with Grade 2 anytime after Chapter 12, Lesson 12-2.

You Will Need

Shell Facts game board

Shell Facts game cards (18)

Teacher's Note: You will need to cut on the dotted cut lines, fold on the solid fold lines, and paste the front and back sides of the cards together for this game.

Shell Facts answer key

or counters (25 for each player)

1 number cube

How to Start

Two Players

Each player tosses the number cube. The player who tosses the lesser number is Player 1 and starts the game.

Player 2 mixes the game cards and places them facedown on the green Card Pile on the game board.

How to Play

Shell Facts is a matching game.

Player 1 takes the top card from the green Card Pile and checks for a match on the shell grid on the game board. A match is made when the addition or multiplication sentence on the card matches either an addition or multiplication sentence on the shell grid. For example, $4 + 4$ would match 2×4.

Player 2 uses the answer key or counters to check Player 1's answer. If it is correct, the card is placed on the matching answer on the shell grid with the picture side up.

If it is not correct, the card is placed on the red Card Pile, and it is Player 2's turn.

Players take turns. If all of the cards on the green Card Pile are used, the cards on the red Card Pile are mixed and placed facedown on the green Card Pile.

The winner is the player who puts the last card on the shell grid to complete the picture.

Answer Key: Shell Facts		
1. 3 x 6	7. 2 x 7	13. 0 + 0 + 0 + 0
2. 7 + 7 + 7	8. 3 x 4	14. 5 + 5 + 5
3. 3 x 2	9. 5 x 0	15. 5 x 4
4. 4 x 1	10. 4 + 4 + 4 + 4	16. 5 x 5
5. 1 + 1 +1 + 1 + 1	11. 6 + 6 + 6 + 6	17. 2 x 6
6. 2 x 5	12. 3 x 3	18. 2 x 0

Variation

After a player matches a multiplication game card with a repeated addition game card, the player must give the answer to the problem.

1.
6 + 6 + 6
Shell Facts
2.
3 × 7
Shell Facts
3.
2 + 2 + 2
Shell Facts
4.
1 + 1 + 1 + 1
Shell Facts
5.
5 × 1
Shell Facts
FOLD

7.

$7 + 7$

Shell Facts

8.

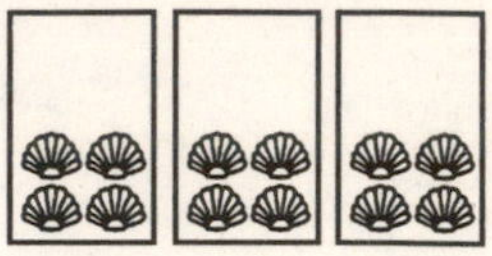

$4 + 4 + 4$

Shell Facts

9.

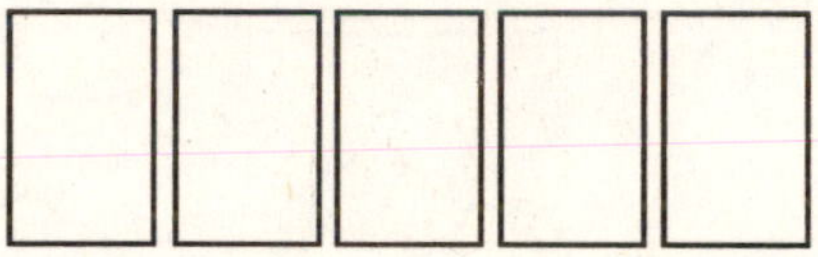

$0 + 0 + 0 + 0 + 0$

Shell Facts

10.

4×4

Shell Facts

11.

4×6

Shell Facts

FOLD

13.
4 × 0
Shell Facts
14.
3 × 5
Shell Facts
15.
4 + 4 + 4 + 4 + 4
Shell Facts
16.
5 + 5 + 5 + 5 + 5
Shell Facts
17.
6 + 6
Shell Facts
FOLD

6.

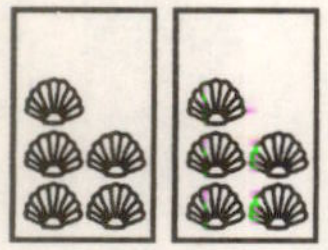

$5 + 5$

Shell Facts

12.

$3 + 3 + 3$

Shell Facts

18.

$0 + 0$

Shell Facts

FOLD